THE
OLD RULES
OF MARKETING
ARE DEAD

THE
OLD RULES
OF MARKETING
ARE DEAD

6 New Rules
to Reinvent Your Brand & Reignite Your Business

TIMOTHY R. PEARSON

New York   Chicago   San Francisco   Lisbon   London   Madrid   Mexico City
Milan   New Delhi   San Juan   Seoul   Singapore   Sydney   Toronto

Copyright © 2011 by Timothy R. Pearson. All rights reserved. Printed in the United
States of America. Except as permitted under the United States Copyright Act of 1976,
no part of this publication may be reproduced or distributed in any form or by any
means, or stored in a database or retrieval system, without the prior written permission
of the publisher.

2 3 4 5 6 7 8 9 10 11 12   QFR/QFR   1 9 8 7 6 5 4 3 2 1 (0-07-176255-8)
1 2 3 4 5 6 7 8 9 10 11 12   QFR/QFR   1 9 8 7 6 5 4 3 2 1 (0-07-178822-0)

ISBN 978-0-07-176255-7 (hardcover)
MHID   0-07-176255-8

ISBN 978-0-07-178822-9 (paperback)
MHID   0-07-178822-0

e-ISBN 978-0-07-176256-4
e-MHID   0-07-176256-6

This publication is designed to provide accurate and authoritative information in regard
to the subject matter covered. It is sold with the understanding that the publisher is
not engaged in rendering legal, accounting, securities trading, or other professional
services. If legal advice or other expert assistance is required, the services of a
competent professional person should be sought.
> —*From a Declaration of Principles Jointly Adopted by a Committee of the
> American Bar Association and a Committee of Publishers and Associations*

Library of Congress Cataloging-in-Publication Data

Pearson, Timothy R.
      The old rules of marketing are dead : 6 new rules to reinvent your brand and
reignite your business / by Timothy R. Pearson.
            p.   cm.
      Includes index.
      ISBN 978-0-07-176255-7 (alk. paper)
      1. Branding (Marketing).   2. Communications.   I. Title.

HF5415.1255.P43   2011
658.8′27—dc22   2010047468

Interior design by THINK Book Works

McGraw-Hill books are available at special quantity discounts to use as premiums and
sales promotions, or for use in corporate training programs. To contact a representative
please e-mail us at bulksales@mcgraw-hill.com.

This book is printed on acid-free paper.

For my parents, Dick and Ramalee Pearson, who taught me about faith and goodness, and the endless possibilities of reinvention; my brother Tom, from whom I learned that intellect, contribution, and daily effort are not only acknowledged, but also rewarded; my brother Philip, who showed me that the ability to create and paint with words is, in fact, art; and my brother David, whom I admire and respect for living a life of honesty, courage, and worthiness.

CONTENTS

ACKNOWLEDGMENTS

In the early spring of 2009 I received an unexpected telephone call from an old acquaintance, Mike Maxsenti, president and publisher of The Place Media. After the normal pleasantries that take place between longtime friends, Mike asked me if I knew of anyone who could serve as a keynote speaker to an important and influential gathering of business executives; leaders of leisure, hospitality, and tourism industries; government representatives; and marketing heads. The topic was to be the reigniting of the Southern California travel and tourism–driven economy in reaction to the Great Recession. I made a couple of initial suggestions of possible candidates, and then Mike posed the real purpose of his call: would I consider being one of the featured speakers? Ultimately, after some initially hesitancy, I ceded to Mike's persistence, and the views and opinions I expressed 60 days later to this engaged and diverse group of individuals brought together by a common purpose would result in this book.

While *The Old Rules of Marketing Are Dead: 6 New Rules to Reinvent Your Brand and Reignite Your Business* has taken more than 10 months to complete, it has as its true gestation 32 years of preparation and groundwork in my experiences with leading advertising agencies and consulting firms as well as with directing marketing, communications, and brand initiatives for both U.S. and global companies. In addition to my own perspectives and outlook, I am very grateful for the contributions of those I have worked with closely over the years. It is impossible to thank each one by name, but I am particularly indebted to those who served as subject matter experts in the review of early drafts of this book.

I want to recognize the important and substantive contributions of Jack Sansolo, retired senior vice president, chief marketing officer, Getty Images, Inc., and former executive vice president, global brand direction, Eddie Bauer LLC; MaryLee Sachs, chairman, Hill & Knowlton USA, and director, Worldwide Marketing Communications Practice, Hill & Knowlton, Inc.; Bruce Barta, executive vice president and group account director, Hill Holliday Advertising; John Copeland, senior expert, marketing and sales practice, McKinsey & Company; Shawn Coyne, co-managing partner, the Coyne Partnership, Inc.; Alfredo Ortiz, principal, Boston Consulting Group; Sean Harper, director, Gupton Marrs International; and Glen Gilbert, former global director, brand management, KPMG, and founder, Inventive Branding, LLC.

I also want to acknowledge Andy Pierce, CAA Sports, Creative Artists Agency, formerly head of corporate consulting at IMG; and Simon Green, literary agent, Creative Artists Agency, who provided invaluable guidance in negotiating a publishing agreement with McGraw-Hill. Equally, I want to express my thanks to Philip Ruppel, president, McGraw-Hill Professional, for his advocacy and initial support; Mary Glenn, associate publisher, McGraw-Hill Professional, for her encouragement and suggestion to focus on reinvention; Stephanie Frerich, acquisition editor, McGraw-Hill Professional, for her many contributions to the negotiation and contractual process; Ron Martirano, senior project editor, McGraw-Hill Professional, for his input and noteworthy involvement in the overall framing and structure of the initial drafts; Charlie Fisher, senior project editor, McGraw-Hill Professional, for his invaluable suggestions and adroit management of (and adherence to) the master production schedule; and Alison Shurtz, copyeditor, for her tireless attention to the final manuscript.

Lastly, I would like to give special acknowledgement to Tom Pearson, retired senior vice president, law and administration, general counsel and secretary, Alliance Resource Partners, L.P., and Jeannette Marsh, director, internal communications, United Healthcare. It would not have been possible to complete my undertaking without their ongoing invaluable support and assistance. This book is as much theirs as it is mine.

A NOTE ABOUT
THE TIMELINE

This book looks at a snapshot in time—a particular period now being called the Great Recession when the necessity of a reinvented and revitalized way of marketing became critically and abundantly clear to many companies and enterprises. The timeline of my writing ended January 26, 2011, when this book was finalized and submitted for publication. Since that time, many of the serious business issues or events cited in this book will undoubtedly have evolved, and unquestionably much will have happened that underscores my assertion that the old rules of marketing are dead and marketing itself needs to be reinvented.

As we ease, slowly and painfully, out of this Great Recession, while much will have fundamentally changed—in fact, it has already—much will have remained the same. Critically, marketing must change with the times, and I believe that the core lessons, tenets, and theories put forth in this book will continue to be relevant regardless of what is yet to come. Simply, those leaders and practitioners of marketing must facilitate and help lead the reinvention of American business in a changed and ever increasingly competitive marketplace because it will be the companies and enterprises that break away from their legacies and reinvent their businesses that will inherit the next era of global commerce.

THE
OLD RULES
OF MARKETING
ARE DEAD

INTRODUCTION

What Memo Did Marketers Miss?

Reinvention is rooted in six key rules that encompass a new way of examining marketing's critical role in contributing profitable sales and increased revenue to a successful company or enterprise.

DID NOT want to write this book. In fact, I avoided sitting down at the desk in my office for several months before I finally was persuaded to begin the time-consuming process of actually putting pen to paper (or, in this instance, fingers to keyboard). The reason for my hesitancy was that while writing has always been, for the most part, relatively easy for me, the potentially controversial topic that I was encouraged to confront was somewhat problematic. That topic: the state of marketing today.

Addressing this required me to not only acknowledge but accept the reality that as a former chief marketing officer and CEO of advertising and consulting companies, the profession that I had spent more than 25 years in was sadly out of touch with the times. Particularly, I now see that my chosen field has been deficient in recognizing the changes brought about by the new technologies and Internet-based tools developed in the first decade of the 21st century; the ready availability of information-rich data and the resulting insights that could be used to exploit changing or evolving business opportunities; and our country's most recent financial struggles, frequently referred to as the Great Recession.

By way of background, the genesis of *The Old Rules of Marketing Are Dead: 6 New Rules to Reinvent Your Brand and Reignite Your Business* came about through a keynote speech that I delivered to a high-profile group of business leaders, government officials, senior marketing professionals, and the heads of leisure, hospitality, and tourism industries in Southern California in April 2009. The speech was titled "The Old Rules Are Dead: 10 Ways to Navigate the Challenges Ahead," and it focused on ways for these leaders and business executives to come to grips with and respond to the devastating impact of the Great Recession on cities, theme parks, hotels, and resort developments located in Los Angeles, Orange, and San Diego counties.

The response to this particular speech was overwhelmingly and universally positive—far more so than I could possibly have imagined. Attendees asked countless questions, wanted copies of the speech, and (surprising at least to me) to know where to find and purchase the then nonexistent book so they could immediately begin to use these concepts to reinvent their businesses, services, and products. Subsequent speeches I made such as "Do or Die: The Reinvention of Marketing" that used the premise that the old ways of marketing have been replaced by new, more up-to-date approaches received the same response. Clearly, I had touched upon the core of the concerns marketers and business leaders had—but were uncertain about or, even worse, afraid to confront. Leaders of all sorts were in search of answers to difficult problems caused by changes that few understood—and even fewer knew how to solve. The world had changed, but unfortunately marketing had not.

Even as I sit writing this extended preamble, it continues to astound me that with all this constant and unrelenting technology-driven change—change that has impacted so many around the world, not only in the developed countries and the emerging BRIC nations (Brazil, Russia, India, and China) but also the third world—one thing has remained firmly rooted and mired in the past: the way products and services are marketed and sold.

Somehow, marketers missed the memo.

Marketing Then

As I began to better understand this new reality and talked to other leaders in business, it became clear to me that the old way of marketing is no longer able to deliver optimal results. Even worse, marketing is not leading the dialogue about reinvention, and, for that reason, it is not (or is no longer) considered vital to many organizations or enterprises.

You are undoubtedly familiar with the old ways of marketing. You were taught them in undergraduate or graduate school, as an intern or first-year junior marketing or sales associate. As a result, you have probably seen the old rules put into practice.

The old way of doing things can be summarized as follows:

>> Budgets define strategy.
>> A brand is just a brand.
>> It's all about the qualitative research.
>> Advertising is the answer.
>> Marketing results cannot be measured.
>> Technology isn't for everyone.

These "rules" were based on a number of widely accepted beliefs, primarily that marketing is more an art than a science. As with most assumptions, these have proven to be untrue, particularly in this technology- and data-rich informational era of the Internet.

Regrettably, from research frameworks and traditional concept development to planning, budgeting, distribution channels, and media placement, marketers have not kept up. In fact, marketing has not advanced in many ways, which may be why chief marketing officers don't get a seat at the leadership table. Bluntly, as a result of the rapid advancements in technology and the depth and breadth of information that is readily—if not instantaneously—available to power and propel profitable sales and increase revenues, marketing should have changed. But it hasn't. It remains rooted in the not-too-distant past.

It's a past that needs to be reexamined and analyzed through the lens of reinvention. More than that, though, marketing is a practice that needs to be reinvented to have a future—one in which this critically important discipline leads instead of fol-lows. Today, to be successful marketers need to change—their approaches, processes, and even their organizations. However, that doesn't mean that all the rules of marketing should be rejected. Many remain valid but need to be reconsidered in light of the changes and advancements that have been made in tech-nologies, media, and channels and the resulting repositories of information readily available through the Internet. This book was created for that reason—to help business leaders and mar-keters reinvent their products and services, and their future.

Marketing Now

Do you remember life before Google?

In an era when new technologies and applications are avail-able daily, Google was a game changer. Google reinvented how people searched for information. No longer did you need to go to the library and find microfiche copies of articles for informa-tion—you could find it, amazingly and quickly, online. All you had to do was type in a few keywords and hit "Search." Almost magically, the information you needed came to you—swiftly, easily, and at no cost. Yes, other aggregators had come before, but none had made the process so accessible, so easy, so quick—or so cool.

Alongside Google, IBM, Microsoft, Apple, Dell, and oth-ers created hardware and software that allowed, initially, for ever-greater productivity. This included one-stop access to office-oriented tools such as Word, PowerPoint, Excel, and the all-important e-mail, the bane (or bonanza, depending on which side you represent) of litigators everywhere because it provides an all-but-permanent record of conversations, exchanges, agree-ments and disagreements, and bargains that serve as the basis of business dealings and transactions.

Access to information beyond the confines of one's desk-top, however, over time became Google's dominant domain and what fueled its meteoric rise in awareness, usage, and market capitalization.

Before Google there really was no single global gateway to the Internet that everyone was both aware of and regularly used—it seemed as though there was no one place to go to get amassed and aggregated information. With its introduction in 1998, Google began to change behavior—and even language—with its amazing search capabilities that delivered fast, accurate, and convenient results. Today, "Googling" is omnipresent. When questions come up, the answers are "Googled"—it's now part of the lexicon. Google is now being chased by Bing, Yahoo!, Ask .com, AltaVista, AOL, and many others, none of which—not even those search engines that predated Google's launch—have gained the usage or the place in the cultural zeitgeist that Google almost immediately captured and continues to hold.

However, Google has one thing going for it that the others don't: its corporate structure. Unlike Bing (created by Microsoft, the behemoth in the computer industry), Google is still flexible enough to respond quickly to and even anticipate or create marketplace needs—sometimes so transparently users don't even realize it.

Google's Impact

Google preconditioned users for Facebook, MySpace, and Twitter in that it taught people to expect instant satisfaction and instant answers as well as offering a way for people to connect with the information they need in an increasingly disconnected and frenetic world. Most important for those in marketing, Google's advertiser-supported model not only changed the way traditional and online marketing was practiced, it reinvented the way people carry out and conduct both personal and professional business and brought forth an explosion of channels and transaction-oriented websites.

Surprisingly, somehow most marketers missed the memo. While consumers, customers, and the marketplace changed, most marketers—and most businesses—did not.

Many companies still practice marketing the same way today as they did in the 1970s and 1980s, clinging to the old ways of working, seemingly not aware of—and definitely not attuned to—this new age of marketing that places a premium on business acumen, strategy, and communications. By doing so, they miss opportunities to drive profitable revenue and they set themselves up for less than optimum performance—if not outright failure.

When business leaders try to get with the new program by talking about leveraging Twitter and Facebook and exploiting new technology channels, most have not done so successfully. If they were being honest, few truly would know what success via social networking even looks like. Business leaders may throw around terms like *SEO* (search engine optimization), but they don't truly understand what it means—to their business and to their marketing efforts.

The New Age of Marketing

The new age of marketing is one in which practices like "behavioral economics" are no longer the primary drivers. According to the *McKinsey Quarterly*, "Long before behavioral economics had a name, marketers were using it. 'Three for the price of two' offers and extended-payment layaway plans became widespread because they worked—*not because marketers had run scientific studies* showing that people prefer a supposedly free incentive to an equivalent price discount or that people often behave irrationally when thinking about future consequences" (emphasis added).[1]

The key take-away from McKinsey's article is "not because marketers had run scientific studies": if marketers don't undertake research or utilize business analytic tools to fully understand the factors that influence and actually cause purchase decisions, how can they truly know that a program worked? Marketing on price point isn't about brand building, and it focuses consumers and customers on cycles when the product or service is on sale. It also isn't very scientific, which at its heart marketing must be. Simply put, by leveraging behavioral economics, marketers were creating commodities, not brands.

Marketing in this new data-abundant, Internet-oriented world order requires more than a shallow or superficial understanding of the customer or consumer—and more than simply "getting on" the new technology. It requires understanding that the old ways of marketing are dead. They can be found stuffed and hanging on the walls of offices around the world. The fundamentals have changed, as have the means and methods to define targets, to create more productive encounters that provide more opportunities to sell, to develop deeper and more significant insights, and to exploit singular points of difference.

Old paradigms must be challenged. There is a new way of doing things, one that, when executed properly and successfully, can help businesses reinvent themselves to win in this new global marketplace. It requires that marketers throw out almost all that they hold dear and embrace technology, a new role, and real accountability—wholeheartedly. Reinvention requires fundamental change.

The Impact of the Great Recession

Change is never easy. Beginning in 2007, as a result of the Great Recession, most marketers and many business leaders found themselves cast adrift, seeking salvation amid a sea of change. And while the government may say the recession ended in June 2009, the reality for many Americans is that it continues—and will continue until the unemployment and poverty rates go down (which, as of this writing, they have not). Only then will the Great Recession be over for Americans. Until then, the landscape for business remains changed and uncertain.

In fact, just about every aspect of American life—both personal and professional—has experienced fundamental change in one form or another since the end of 2007 and the beginning of the end of the housing bubble and the ensuing financial crisis. These sweeping changes have, in many cases, left many people (and many leaders) numb and in search of answers and new solutions, while others have been left angry—and have expressed their anger through the various Tea Party movements that have rocked politics. Simply put, for many, the status quo is unacceptable.

But new solutions are slow in coming in a world that many believe has changed for the long term. According to a *McKinsey Quarterly* survey published in September 2010:

> Notably, the share of respondents expecting better conditions in six months is lower than it was a year ago: 55 percent now, compared with 61 percent in September 2009. Furthermore, optimism on the current state of the economy compared with six months earlier started to fall in June and has taken a sharp dive in the past month. Compared with August, 10 percentage points fewer say the economy is better now. The slide is particularly notable in North America, where the share of respondents who say conditions are better has fallen 16 percentage points. After two years, it appears that at many companies, ongoing economic uncertainty is being balanced with more rigorous planning and execution of everything from daily operations to M&A. Many companies are smaller, and, at many, morale is damaged.[2]

The Aftermath

As a result, it seems that businesses, like their customers, are in search of remedies and a path or way out as well. While many companies pride themselves on being nimble and innovative, able to meet any challenge presented and come out stronger, this particular point of time in history seems to have shaken that faith.

In the face of this uncertainty, the idea of reinvention is hard to embrace. Reinvention requires considered risk. And, as a consequence of the Great Recession and the risk-taking by many financial institutions that caused or at least contributed to it, today this type of change can be seen as perilous. Generally speaking, taking risks is not encouraged, let alone rewarded, by large corporations and businesses overall. Institutionalizing a culture that embraces changes to business practices, operating systems and procedures, and new processes is even harder. That is why reinvention must be the byword for this era—the change it requires is actually a return to the core of what can make a business great.

I served as vice chairman and global managing partner, brand management, marketing and communications for KPMG LLP during a decade that saw tremendous change in the professional services and consulting industries—the implosion of Andersen, the global merger of Price Waterhouse and Coopers & Lybrand, the creation—and ultimate failure from an ill-conceived and poorly executed global expansion—of BearingPoint, the acquisition of Ernst & Young's global consulting practice by Capgemini, IBM's purchase of PricewaterhouseCoopers' consulting unit, and the imposition of new regulations and creation of new regulatory bodies such as the Public Company Accounting Oversight Board (PCAOB). In that leadership role, I saw firsthand how global industries and companies react when change is imposed from the outside.

As one of the remaining Big Four global accounting firms, KPMG was open to transformation and reinvention, but it was never easy. For example, when Gene O'Kelly was elected chairman of KPMG in the United States in 2002 (he served until he retired for health reasons in 2005), one of the goals during his tenure was to make the firm an employer of choice within five years. At the time, human capital was all-important because long-term aggressive market share growth was limited by constrained capacity. There simply weren't enough people to do all the work that clients and prospects were demanding. Becoming an employer of choice required real cultural change from the ground up. It required an internally driven approach that touched every aspect of how KPMG went about its business. It also required that, as a firm, we understood the core essence of KPMG.

That center, heart and core, shared by the 2,000-plus partners and 20,000-plus professionals of KPMG was an intense competitive drive and a desire to perform and win in the marketplace. So, at the national level, we devised a plan that created a framework for becoming an employer of choice, using the core essence of the firm's brand as the foundation. Simply stated, we made becoming an employer of choice a challenge. This framework was flexible enough to allow for customization—which local office could make its employees feel most valued, which partners best embodied the spirit of employer of choice, and so on. And we leveraged success stories to increase awareness and participation by all 22,000-plus individuals.

Importantly, these efforts were not one-offs—partners and employees didn't simply get an award or trophy and then go back to the old ways of doing things. The firm held both partners and employees accountable for what would become a true change in culture by evaluating their efforts using GE's nine-box methodology, a balanced, effective performance management and standardized measurement methodology, to ensure their commitment and performance, and then rewarding them based on long-term contribution and achievement.

By knowing the target audience, creating a strategy that both appealed to and leveraged employees' strengths, and making change rewarding in the aggregate as well as at the individual level, KPMG became an employer of choice (as measured by its appearance on *Fortune*'s "100 Best Companies to Work For" list) in three years, not five—and reinvented its culture. The reinvention of KPMG had a direct and singular impact on performance as the firm became the industry growth leader during this period, increasing its U.S. audit market share from 11.8 percent to 23 percent.

Cultural change takes time and requires a spirit of reinvention. There must be an understanding that while change may be difficult, it is also necessary. Americans are undergoing changes that many still don't completely understand or embrace as a result of the Great Recession and the corresponding implosion of the job and housing markets that cost many their nest eggs and sense of financial safety and security. These changes have created a new, difficult landscape, one that requires leaders and marketers to do something that is embodied in the American spirit—reinvention.

The Reinvention of Marketing

These days *reinvention* may be seen as a very "New Agey" term that more often than not speaks to how individuals "make themselves over" to meet and confront the next stage or phase in their lives. That same conceptual construction is also directly applicable to brands, products, and services—and to marketing as a whole.

For the purposes of this book, here is the simplified definition of reinvention that we will be working with: *Reinvention is the process by which a brand, its core essence, and its key attributes are examined, and through the rigorous application of market-based data (as well as applied findings and customer and consumer insights), the next phase or evolution of the brand that capitalizes on those qualities and optimizes profitable revenue is determined—all while staying true to the essential core nature of the product or service.*

The Rules of Reinvention

Reinvention begins at a brand's core essence and is constructed from there. It is not change that is artificially created or imposed externally, nor is it change for its own sake. Rather, it is rooted in six essential and critical rules that encompass a new way of examining and scrutinizing marketing and undertaking and optimizing growth initiatives.

These rules, along with the principles that constitute them, also serve to organize the book you are currently holding. Over the following pages, this book will delve into and explore six fundamental rules applied by way of 23 principles of reinvention to demonstrate how to advance and bring marketing into the 21st century. More important, it will show that it is crucial to reinvent and strategically position marketing as a business partner to allow it to accomplish its imperative goals: to drive profitable sales, create growing brands, and increase market share.

The rules are as follows:

Rule One: The Core Is Everything

Reinvention begins with understanding just what a product or service is at its core. More often than not, lost in the go-to-market processes and sales methodologies is the need to define the true core essence of the product or service that is being marketed. Knowing and understanding that core essence not only makes a product or service more relevant, it also creates a touchstone for all the work that will follow. Everything that is undertaken must be true to the essence.

Rule Two: You Have Nothing Without the Foundation

Reinvention is not an art, nor is it a science—it's both. Once the core essence of a brand, product, or service has been determined, it's necessary to develop the foundation for creating and reinventing the brand. In marketing, there is a tendency to think of branding as "building a house." This tenet deals with creating the architecture and laying the foundation for the brand house— that's part of the science.

Rule Three: There Are Many Choices but Only One Customer

Reinvention does a product or service no good if it's not effectively and efficiently conveyed and shared with the key audience—the potential buyer or acquirer of that product or service. Having "built the house," it's crucial to determine the plan for going to market and creating the metrics to ensure or exceed a targeted return on investment. Here, the focus is on planning, creating consistency, developing messaging, and determining channels to reach that key audience—the customer.

Rule Four: Do The Right Things for the Right Reasons

Reinvention requires an understanding of the circumstance and context in which the product or service is taken to market. There are no shortcuts or easy fixes. Before putting the brand house "up for sale," there is a need to ensure there are no unexpected or unanticipated barriers or constraints. These could involve regulatory issues; reputational concerns; customer, client, or prospect relationships; and even entering into partnerships that elevate or accelerate acceptance and purchase of the product or service.

Rule Five: Infrastructure Is More than Just Pipes

Reinvention begins with a product or service, but it does not end there. It directly impacts and shapes the operating infrastructure that supports it. As the product or service is taken to market, it becomes important to focus on the type of support necessary for the successful implementation of the plan. There is no "magic bullet," but there are avenues that must be explored and optimized, requiring a clear and undiluted understanding of the role marketing is to play in the company or enterprise and the creation of the right type of marketing organization.

Rule Six: Lead and Others Will Follow

Marketing must demonstrate leadership to ensure that reinvention is not only seen as contributing to the bottom line, but in fact does so successfully. Beyond that, it must continue to contribute time and time again over a long period with ever-increasing efficiency and effectiveness to drive profitable revenue growth.

The Business of Reinvention

As a practice essential to a company or enterprise, marketing has failed in many ways. The key failure is one of accountability. By not producing hard metrics on how it contributes to the bottom line, and by positioning itself as more of an art than a science, marketing has left itself open to being viewed as a cost center that isn't vital to a company's ongoing success. While nothing is further from the truth, without providing proof of both contributing to and exceeding a targeted return on investment, marketing sets itself up for skepticism if not outright cynicism, disbelief, and failure.

In a time when consumers and customers are ever more careful in evaluating, distinguishing, and selecting from among the countless choices presented to them, marketing is now more than ever very serious business, and the role of the chief marketing officer (CMO) or chief development officer (CDO) is crucial.

Another breakdown of marketing is one of leadership. One aspect of leadership is an understanding of—and curiosity about—the future that allows leaders to anticipate change. Too many marketers missed the importance of the "green" movement and have had to play catch-up in understanding how "green" can differentiate and advance a company, product, or service in the marketplace. Additionally, as of this writing the idea of "sustainability" is something the vast majority of marketing professionals have not embraced. It's a hard concept to comprehend, let alone communicate or market, but it is one that can further differentiate and predispose the purchase of a product or service with its many audiences because of the heightened consumer awareness brought about by increased media coverage and the controversial government regulation of industries that are viewed as contributing to global warming and the ongoing buildup of human-related greenhouse gases.

Marketing must provide leadership in its most traditional sense. An overused word but an underpracticed concept, *leadership* requires guidance, management, and rigorous assessment. Leadership drives breakthrough performance, which should be the hallmark of marketing. The art of reinvention must be integrated astutely with the data-driven science of marketing in this technology-oriented world where change is a given and a constant. And that takes leadership.

Marketing drives business by creating perceived value; this leads to trial and ultimately to the purchase and continued purchase (or repurchase) of a product or service. Businesses only make money when they sell something, not when they manufacture something—you can't sell something unless you market it successfully.

The Old Way Versus the New Way

The key difference between the old and new ways of marketing is that the new way recognizes that marketing must be applied strategically, in the context of today's technology and data-centered world. The new way also more often than not requires marketers to reinvent their products and services.

As the president and chief executive officer of a nationally recognized management consulting firm that specialized in business and brand strategy, consumer and business insights, and marketing best practices and organizational design, I saw firsthand many Fortune 1000 companies and their marketing executives simply throw dollars at the marketplace without thoroughly and completely understanding their brands. These C-level executives were not looking to the core of their products' or services' essence. Their marketing organizations were not leveraging and exploiting today's technology-driven and data-rich environment or the real insights and reasons why a customer or consumer makes the decision to purchase. Rather, they continued to do things as they always had—maybe changing the packaging in an attempt to attract new customers. Those are among some of the reasons their products and services were so commoditized and their go-to-market approaches suboptimized.

In this new world order, marketers have no choice but to reinvent their brands to keep pace with the changing marketplace. They need to know what those brands are at the core because if they don't, in all likelihood target audiences won't know either. The result of failure at any level is that audiences simply won't buy the products or services—initially or with the frequency that the company or enterprise desires. Remember, the all-critical goal is profitable sales, growing brands, and increased market share.

That memo marketers missed? It's the one that requires marketers to break out of old routines by:

>> Applying the six rules of reinvention
>> Viewing what they do as essential to the business
>> Recognizing that marketing is accountable for results
>> Providing leadership, not simply following the leader (Often the leader stands alone; that can be daunting, but it is ultimately rewarding—when done correctly.)
>> Understanding that businesses make money only when they sell something, and you can't sell something unless you successfully market it first

This book is the follow-up to the memo marketers missed. Its intent is to serve as a road map and guide for business leaders and owners, marketers and sales executives, and all other individuals interested in the survival, growth, and future prosperity of a business or enterprise. In a world of unrelenting change driven by forces including technology, economics, and regulation, its messages cannot be missed again because the successful reinvention of businesses and brands depends upon it.

THE CORE of a brand is its essence—what it is at its heart. It is the unique differentiator and distinctiveness that attracts buyers and consumers time and time again, building brand preference and customer loyalty.

A brand's core is an intangible, and it's an emotional connection to the consumer or customer based on preferences and experience.

Critically, by moving away from this core, companies and enterprises can over time harm and damage their brands and the relationship with their targeted audiences—in doing so limiting their potential and sacrificing revenue growth and market opportunities. However, that doesn't mean that brands shouldn't evolve. In fact, a brand must evolve in order to survive and thrive in a constantly changing environment.

A product or service must be constantly reinvented to optimize growth and market penetration—all the while remaining true to its core.

A Brand's Essence Says It All

Reinvention begins with understanding just what a
product or service is—and what it is not.

More and more, from a wellness and physical fitness perspective, doctors, therapists, and personal trainers focus first on the core—the muscles that provide strength, balance, and stability to the body—as they work to rehabilitate and strengthen the body. They've got good reason to do so, as core development strengthens the back while improving balance, coordination, and cardiac and circulatory function. This analogy can be easily transferred to marketing and the absolute necessity of knowing and understanding the core essence of a brand—and the resulting benefits derived by the company or enterprise.

Before they can create a marketing strategy, messaging, and tactics, before they can introduce a product or service to the marketplace, before they can do anything, marketers must know what their product or service stands for—its core essence—and how to position or present the brand to the target audience. Reinvention begins with a brand's core essence. A brand's essence "captures compelling points of difference; guides brand strategy; may be aspirational; and, communicates direction to internal stakeholders."[1]

The Core

Reinvention starts with the core of the brand. What exactly is that brand? Is it, like Levis, the all-American, classic jean epitomizing effortless cool? Or is it like Avis—number 2, but trying harder? Is it the new Holiday Inn, which offers everything a business traveler could want at a low price point—including a comfortable bed, free Wi-Fi, and free breakfast? Is it Starbucks, the popularizer of designer coffee at a designer price? Or is it Dunkin Donuts, simply good coffee at a good price? If as a leader or marketer, you can't sum up what the core essence of the brand is, or if you have to commission a study to uncover it, the brand is probably in trouble. And if internal stakeholders can't define the brand, the product or service is most likely in even bigger danger.

Often, as products or services extend their reach, the core essence of the brand gets diffused and muddied or, even worse, lost. However, the core essence is what makes the brand unique, so as it gets further away from its core, the brand is at risk of losing its differentiation and its distinctiveness. That loss makes a brand a commodity—something consumers or customers buy on price point, not desire. The brand goes from a "have to have" to a "don't need," especially in an economy where customers and consumers' shopping habits are focused on sales, not simply buying. When that happens, the brand has lost its uniqueness and individuality and is ripe for reinvention.

The Criteria a Core Essence Must Meet

When determining the core essence of a product or service, recognize that it is often intangible. The best core essences are also:

>> **Single-minded:** You and your internal stakeholders should be able to describe your brand essence in a few words—it must be that well thought out and true.
>> **Emotional:** An essence is based on how the consumer feels about the product.
>> **Unique:** The essence of a brand is how it is different from competitors in the same category.
>> **Experiential:** The essence describes how consumers or buyers experience the brand.

>> **Believable:** The essence must be credible.
>> **Unchanging:** The core essence must be sustainable over time.
>> **Meaningful:** The essence should be important to your target market.
>> **Scalable:** You will need to grow your brand, so your essence must be able to encompass the brand as it attracts a broader and larger base.

The Core of a Service

Often, marketers that are in the business of taking services to the public—from consulting to financial to professional services and others too numerous to describe—don't think they have to worry about core essence. This is another mistake, one that many marketers make. Everything that is sold—be it a product or a service—has a core essence. It has to in order to have points of differentiation from the competition.

Recently, the consulting firm I led took on the project of helping a major insurer embed its essence across its federated companies. The insurer first surveyed key stakeholders to determine what customers and others thought about its brand in comparison to its competitors. As a result of this in-depth study, the company was able to discover key points of parity and points of differentiation for its brand. For marketers, these are essential tools. Points of parity refer to where the field is level—basically, areas where all the brands in the market are considered equal. Points of differentiation are imperative—they are the ways that your brand, be it a product or service, is unlike the competition.

These points of differentiation helped define what customers viewed as the core essence of the brand and led to the creation of a brand positioning, used, in this instance, primarily for internal purposes. That positioning was based on the points of parity (trust, choice, and leader), as well as on the key point of differentiation (advisor) that the company's research had uncovered. As insurers enter into a world of ever-greater government regulation, this proprietary positioning will help the company differentiate itself in the marketplace. In an industry like insurance, where companies more often than not seem interchangeable to the public, this positioning will set the company apart.

Brand Essence Versus Brand Promise

A brand's essence is intangible: it's an emotional connection to the consumer or customer based on preferences and experience. It's very different from a brand promise, which is the contract you make with your customers, often delivered in an advertising tagline.

According to McKinsey & Company, "As companies lose the ability to differentiate their brands based on functional attributes, they must focus on process and relationship benefits, such as ease of ordering or responsiveness to customer requests. Thus, frontline employees must understand and deliver the right brand promise to the customer."[2]

Take, for example, FedEx. At its core, the company is perhaps the best logistical operation in the world. However, its brand promise is summed up in its original advertising campaign slogan: "Absolutely, positively overnight." All of its employees were expected to keep this promise, and it became the differentiator between FedEx and its then only global competitor, the United States Postal Service. (Interestingly, in September 2010 UPS introduced a new company-wide campaign, "We Love Logistics.") Since FedEx executed on its original brand promise and enjoyed first-mover advantage as well, it too has entered the lexicon as a means for sending a package overnight—the public will often say "FedEx" even if they mean UPS or one of its other competitors. Similarly, Xerox to this day—as it undergoes a reinvention to a business process and document management services company—is still known as "the copier people." Unfortunately, it is burdened by the legacy disadvantage of being associated with paper duplication in a digital age.

The Core Creates Positioning

Once you know a brand's core, the brand positioning can be created. To construct this positioning, you need to understand exactly where you want this product or service to take your company or enterprise over time, and you must clearly define what success looks like.

Twice a year, fashion designers gather in New York, London, and Paris to present their haute couture lines—which in many cases are loss leaders. In fact, it is not the Fashion Week presentations that actually make money for designers; it's the accessories—shoes, handbags, and jewelry—the line extensions that represent their brand at a more "affordable" price than the couture lines.

Not all designers are willing or able to create these affordable brand extensions. Take, for example, Christian Lacroix, a designer beloved by fashion editors, including the one perceived as the most powerful, *Vogue*'s Anna Wintour. Lacroix's fashion house never made money in its 32-year history, and it went bankrupt in 2009.[3] However, while profitability may have been a goal of the company that owned the Lacroix fashion house, it was not necessarily the core of his business. For him, and other talented and creative designers like him, the motivation is the act of creating beautiful, opulent clothing that drives or changes an industry. While Lacroix's couture fashions were not affordable by any measure, his creations directly impacted what women wore—he was widely viewed as being the creator of the "pouf" style of gown that graces red carpets and formal events to this day.

Knowing your core essence is the starting point for a brand's potential success. While many people would judge Lacroix a business failure, he remains an extremely successful designer and is judged so by his peers. This essence—the heart of your brand—will help you create your positioning, but it will not guarantee a successful business in and of itself.

Knowing your vision—where you want to go—is another aspect of creating a positioning. The venture and at-risk capital businesses that invested in Lacroix should have taken to heart his statement of his vision: "I want to get back to the position where the couture becomes a kind of laboratory of ideas, the way it was with Schiaparelli 40 years ago."[4] Lacroix knows who he is at his core—and it's not a businessman.

The vision is not where you want your brand to be in a year; rather, it is where or what you want it to be in 5 or 10 years or longer. Once you have defined what success looks like and what your vision is, you can begin creating your brand positioning. This will define your marketing strategy.

It's Not Easy

Kevin Keller, a recognized brand expert and the E. B. Osborn Professor of Marketing at the Tuck School of Business at Dartmouth, puts it best when he talks about the difficulty of brand positioning: "Competitive brand positioning is hard work. Many brands falter sooner than they should; some don't even make it out of the gate."[5]

According to Keller, there are five pitfalls to watch out for while positioning a brand:

1. Know your essence. "Companies sometimes try to build brand awareness before establishing a clear brand position. You have to know who you are before you can convince any-one of it," Keller says.[6]
2. Sell customers what they want to buy. According to Keller, "Companies often promote attributes that consumers don't care about."[7]
3. Find unique points of differentiation and focus your mar-keting on those that others can't easily copy. "Positioning needs to keep competitors out, not draw them in. A brand that claims to be the cheapest or the hippest is likely to be leapfrogged."[8]
4. Never underestimate the power of your essence. Stick to it, no matter what the competition does. Keller cites the following: "General Mills used the insight that consumers

viewed honey as more nutritious than sugar to successfully introduce the Honey Nut Cheerios product-line extension. A key competitor, Post, decided to respond by repositioning its Sugar Crisp brand, changing the name to Golden Crisp and dropping the Sugar Bear character as spokesman. But the repositioned brand didn't attract enough new customers, and its market share was severely diminished."[9]

5. Remember that brand positioning is a tough task. "Once you've found one that works, you may need to find a modern way to convey the position, but think hard before you alter it."[10]

Positioning: What Appeals to Consumers or Customers

While architecture is the structure of the "brand house," positioning can be seen (to carry the analogy forward) as those elements that attract the buyer to come in and see the house. It's the memory that is evoked when the buyer thinks about the house, or brand, later. Consumers or prospects need reasons, both functional and emotional, to buy a product or service. The positioning of a product or service provides these reasons.

When I was appointed by KPMG as the firm's first externally recruited chief marketing officer, the firm had not had a unified global brand positioning since its founding by William Peat (the *P* in KPMG) in 1870. At the time I joined the firm in 1998, accounting firms were known for their sameness and opaqueness. Their primary products, the audit attestation and certification they provided for large companies, were largely not understood by anyone other than accounting and financial experts.

With insights gleaned from extensive and exhaustive global quantitative research, we crafted and implemented a clear, simple positioning and undertook a first-ever brand advertising campaign (launched as "It's Time for Clarity") to reinforce that positioning. Most important, the positioning required a simpler, more direct means of communicating with our various constituencies.

Elements of a Brand

As the strategy is created, it helps to keep in mind the primary elements of a brand, all of which should be accounted for in the strategic marketing plan. These elements are:

>> **Core essence:** The "nucleus" of the brand: Who are you?
>> **Architecture:** Specific benefits the brand delivers: What do people buy?
>> **Positioning and value proposition:** Understanding what motivates consumers or customers within a defined competitive space: Why do people buy your brand?
>> **Reputation:** The brand's perceived ability to deliver its value proposition: What do people say about your brand?

Core Essence: An Example

Let's look at how one well-known brand answers these questions.

>> **Core essence**
  > The necessities of life, and more, at a discount
>> **Architecture**
  > Cost-effectiveness
  > Range of brands
  > Size of stores; more space, more products
  > Generic drugs at affordable prices
  > Customer service
  > Special in-store savings
>> **Positioning and value proposition**
  > Save money, live better
>> **Reputation**
  > Good, cost-effective products, especially in a recession
  > Issues with sweatshops and unions have not affected sales.

This brand is, of course, Sam Walton's Wal-Mart. Wal-Mart understands its essence, and, with minor exceptions, has stuck to it and not strayed over the years. That's a lesson all marketers must learn and bear in mind when the temptation to wander beckons. Once marketers can answer all these questions, then and only then can a marketing strategy be created.

REMEMBER

- Reinvention starts with the core. Understanding a brand's core essence is essential to creating a marketing strategy as well as an enduring brand.
- Brand architecture gives consumers and customers reasons for buying a product or service.
- Positioning is the appeal a brand has to its customers or consumers.
- Positioning is at the heart of strategy.

The Customer Really Does Know Best

Innovation is overused by marketers and often fails. Your products and services must return to their core essence to reinvent these brands to grow revenue profitably.

n 1994, the *McKinsey Quarterly* stated the following: "The past decade has not been kind to marketing. Leading packaged goods companies—long viewed as the best marketers—have been unable to count on their marketing departments for innovation and growth. As a result, their CEOs have had to look instead to operations and finance to increase profitability by cutting costs, eliminating marginal products, and 'reengineering' the supply chain. In their view, the blame for marketing's failure lies squarely at the feet of the brand management system—a system that may have helped companies like P&G achieve spectacular earnings growth during the 1950s, 1960s, and 1970s, but that has long since shown itself unable to cope with today's complex marketing landscape."[1]

The authors of the article, while not anticipating the pending burgeoning age of the Internet and the necessity for reinvention brought about by the events of the initial decade of the 21st century, concluded, "The hardest challenge may be instilling a new marketing culture. Making the transition from a relatively simple structure to one in which process-based teams, dispersed throughout their organization, deliver value to consumers and customers will test the beliefs of even the best marketing companies. Those that meet the challenge, however, will enjoy an important competitive advantage—one that will translate into an increased share of market surplus for years to come."[2]

What McKinsey doesn't talk about is the state of the actual practice of marketing. To mask deficiencies and hide the lack of understanding of the true role of marketing, many marketers turned to innovation in the 1990s. Brand innovation is based on the idea that marketers know better than their target audiences what the target wants. This approach mistakes innovation for something it's not, when most often it is simply off track. In of itself, innovation is defined as "the act or process of inventing or introducing something new."[3] The poster child for this type of innovation is, of course, New Coke. It's a story that has been told before, but it requires retelling through the perspective of reinvention.

The Perils of Innovation

Let's admit it—there are few things more American than Coca-Cola. First introduced in 1886, Coca-Cola glass bottles as well as the red and white aluminum Coke cans are icons in the pantheon of consumer brands. They are easily recognizable, whether in a general store in Okoboji, Iowa, or a bar in Wiesbaden, Germany. And, for a long time, they were considered as American as the proverbial apple pie.

The Coca-Cola formula is a heavily guarded trade secret known only to a few insiders. Coke's unique flavor brought the taste of home to soldiers in World Wars I and II and many conflicts thereafter. Its popularity speaks to the globalization of American brands and the expansionist strategies of consumer products in the late 20th century.

Today, there are few places in the world where travelers don't see billboards with the iconic red and white Coke logo, or where you can't get a Coke. And no matter where you go, if you say "Coke" you're understood—it's one of those words that remain the same in any language.

Although it is iconic, however, Coca-Cola is a brand subject to the vagaries of consumer taste, and in the early 1980s it saw its market share falling in the face of the Pepsi Challenge. The company's response was a shocker: it reformulated its classic Coca-Cola into New Coke, with a new recipe and a different taste.

With the introduction of New Coke—the name itself a nod to innovation—the original was removed from the marketplace in the United States to underscore the point that New Coke was the present and the future of the company. Coke's longtime tagline, "The Real Thing . . . Coke Is . . . That's the way it should be . . . Coca-Cola," known to all from television advertising, was, it seemed, no longer true.

Coke did not make this change in a vacuum. It had undertaken testing with numerous focus groups, all of which overwhelmingly preferred the taste of New Coke. However, research participants' stated preference did not translate into purchase— what people say is not necessarily an indication of how they will act. That is why the adage "Actions speak louder than words" is true. (This will be further explored in Principle #10: "Do As I Do, Not As I Say.")

And consumers' actions resonated deeply with the Coca-Cola Company. Seventy-seven days after the rollout of New Coke, it was back to the future with the reintroduction of Coca-Cola Classic. Over time, New Coke disappeared, a failure of epic proportions. And the deep emotional connection between Coke and its public seemed for many to go with it.

Around the same time, Coke introduced one of its first flavored options, Cherry Coke. This quiet introduction's success was lost in the uproar over New Coke. However, Cherry Coke was everything that New Coke wasn't: it was an organic outgrowth of the existing emotional connection between consumers and the company that built on Coke's core essence. It was, simply, a nuanced reinvention of Coke—the commercialization of an existing behavior rather than a breakthrough innovation.

Consumers actually created cherry Cokes—at soda fountains and in diners of the earlier part of the 20th century, where the original Coke was mixed with cherry syrup at the point of sale, becoming popular with both kids and their parents. The surprise is that it took Coca-Cola until the 1980s to create a store version of something that had, organically, become so widespread. What is unsurprising is that Cherry Coke was successful—there was a built-in relationship with consumers that established a predisposition to purchase the new product.

Some would say that while Coke has regained its market share and even showed modest single-digit growth during the 1990s, it has not regained its emotional connection to the consumer. Given that, today, in Coke's backyard in Atlanta, Pepsi-Cola is widely available (which it wouldn't be if it weren't selling), that would seem to be true.

Innovation and Reinvention

Why would such an iconic brand innovate? Simply because innovation—finding new, creative solutions to business problems—is rewarded. Companies recognize that they are mired in the same ways of doing things, so they reward those who think "outside the box." However, "outside the box" thinking often isn't linked to consumer preferences or even to the core essence of a brand. It's based on the notion that the company knows what consumers want from the brand better than its customers do, so they can do whatever they want since it's best for both the brand and its users.

What this type of approach fails to take into account is the emotional connection consumers make to the brands they prefer. Americans in particular are invested in Coca-Cola. From an emotional perspective, Coke is tied to typical all-American activities—picnics, ball games, movies . . . it brings to mind friends and family. "New Coke" disrupted that emotional connection like an unexpected death or a messy divorce. It is not surprising that Coke went back to its classic formulation, but the damage had been done to its once pristine corporate image. More important, damage had also been done to the inherent trust its customers had in the brand.

Despite the lessons of the epic New Coke failure, marketers continue to innovate. Why? Because they don't realize that the rules have changed.

The new rule in this new world is—*reinvent*.

Reinvention as Transformation

Renovation. For many, that term brings to mind months of transforming their house into a newer and, in an ideal world, better home. Renovation, like innovation, is costly (although generally less so), and it is almost always significantly more expensive than contemplated. Often the results are disappointing and the new house isn't really a better home, just a hodgepodge of different architectural styles and motifs. Or, even worse, it can produce a reconstituted "McMansion"—the monstrosities that are rife in many suburbs today. They are big houses, but not really great homes for living.

The better way is to reinvent. You don't tear the house down, you reenvision it. You preserve the core—the parts of the original edifice that make it unique—while you expand the house consistent with the architectural guidelines implicit in, and integral to, the original structure. New entryways are created or walls are demolished to open new living areas, but all in keeping with the core of the original home. It's more than just the cosmetics of renovation—more than simply refinishing cabinets, uncovering hardwood floors, repainting bedrooms, and re-landscaping the front and back yards. It takes the changes in today's lifestyles and advancements in in-home technologies into consideration, but the home's architectural integrity remains unchanged. It stays a home—not just a house.

That sense of newness and comfort is what marketers must try to recapture when reinventing a brand. Marketers know that the only constant is change, so there is a need to constantly refresh and update brands. Customers or consumers, however, become used to seeing their favorite products one way and can react unexpectedly to something different.

Tropicana learned this firsthand when it changed its iconic "orange with a straw through it" symbol to a glass of orange juice. Consumers reacted immediately—and badly. What the company saw as a means of refreshing its branding, its customers saw as a loss of character. The core of the brand—fresh taste—had been replaced, in consumers' minds, by something generic. They didn't like it, and they made their preferences known.

Neil Campbell, president at Tropicana North America in Chicago, part of PepsiCo Americas Beverages, announced Tropicana's retreat, saying, "The criticism is being heeded because it came . . . from our most loyal consumers." Campbell went on to note how Tropicana had "underestimated the deep emotional bond" that their customers had with the original packaging.[4] (Once again, this will be explored further in Principle #10: "Do as I Do, Not as I Say.")

In this case, Tropicana was attempting to grow horizontally, not vertically, by introducing a less caloric orange juice. But that news got lost in the rebranding of the packaging. A smart move was overshadowed by one that was not so smart. And the introduction of a new product—a "diet" orange juice—got lost in a controversy over packaging. However, by moving quickly, Tropicana managed to minimize the damage.

Miller, by comparison, got horizontal growth right. The core essence of Miller Lite can be summed up in its advertising positioning "Great Taste, Less Filling." That positioning harkens back to research that found that as baby boomers got older, they were concerned about their weight, but they didn't want to give up their beer. Miller's positioning captured both emotional concerns—the beer retained its taste while reducing the ingredients that could make consumers fat.

Recognizing the rising popularity of a competitor, Corona, Miller in 2007 introduced its own chelada beer, Miller Chill. The taste was slightly different, with a hint of lime and maybe something else a little exotic, which appealed to the broadening tastes of the American populace, who enjoy a variety of Mexican and Latin flavors. And the positioning was that of a brand extension: "The unique taste of light beer and lime" (the beer originally had 110 calories but was reintroduced in 2010 with 100 calories).

The introduction of Miller Chill was an immediate success for Miller. According to the *Milwaukee-Wisconsin Journal Sentinel*, "In supermarkets, Chill is outselling such established brands as Dos Equis, Michelob Light, Heineken Light, Beck's, Blue Moon, Samuel Adams Boston Lager and Rolling Rock," according to data from AC Nielsen.

Miller president and chief executive officer Tom Long noted that Chill "taps into consumer preferences for specialty beers." Long cited the "Latinization" of the United States as part of the influence for the initiative.

The move worked, as Miller has since gone on to provide data suggesting repeat buys by Chill customers, as well as "getting 50% of its sales volume from new beer drinkers" and "30% of the sales volume . . . from beer drinkers who normally drink less profitable mainstream brands."[5]

For Miller, this reinvented "new" product grew its brand positioning horizontally—it's an extension of the well-known brand—while introducing it to new customers. Simply stated, it held its base while extending and broadening both its appeal and its reach. And it remained true to its core. (Unfortunately, even with first-mover advantage, Miller's success also awoke a long-sleeping giant—Budweiser—which has used superior promotional leverage and media weight to introduce Bud Lite Lime and ultimately capture the majority of the Latinized beer market.)

In a case like Miller's, reinvention is about recognizing latent opportunities. It requires an understanding of your target consumer's changing needs. As people age, their lives and tastes tend to broaden and diversify. Reinvention recognizes that people change, and as they do, their emotional connection to the brands they love changes. So brands must expand, organically and horizontally, to meet these changing needs if they wish to retain—and grow—their connection with the consumers or customers. But their core does not change.

If, however, a marketer wishes to create a new relationship with a new consumer or customer, then innovation can be the correct—although higher-risk—course. In this case, a marketer must use competitive intelligence or company-based consumer or customer insights to create a product or service. Often, this product or service may provide some cost savings and incremental improvements in the bottom line or in market share, but it won't create a sustainable competitive advantage.

Choosing Reinvention

It would seem, then, that most marketers would choose to retain the base they have already nurtured and created. They would choose to reinvent. So why don't they reinvent their brands more often? Or, simply, why haven't they?

Unfortunately, marketers, while they have good intentions, are more often than not misguided. They believe innovation is a response to consumer or customer needs.

Over the past few decades, the National Association for Stock Car Auto Racing (NASCAR) has been called the fastest-growing sport in the United States. For 36 weekends a year it attracts up to 150,000 spectators, considered among the most brand loyal in sports.

Yet as the economy imploded in 2008, so did NASCAR's economic health. Sponsorships dried up, and there was a drop in attendance and in television viewing. Even the stars of the sport —Jeff Gordon and Tony Stewart, both former champions—had trouble attracting sponsorships for the 2011 season, as longtime advertisers—DuPont, a 20-year sponsor of Gordon, and Old Spice, a longtime sponsor of Stewart—chose to leave the sport.

Some might have attributed this implosion in sponsorship and attendance only to the economic impact of the Great Recession on NASCAR's fan base, but a closer look demonstrates that, concurrent with the recession, attempts at innovation failed. Some of this innovation was needed and long overdue because it related to the drivers' safety and the overall safety practices of the sport. However, much like Tropicana, NASCAR made changes without taking its fan base into consideration—and in many ways is paying for it in a drop-off in support.

Over the past few years, NASCAR's leaders put in place a number of innovative new rules that they believed would make the sport safer. This included developing the "Car of Tomorrow," which incorporated a number of improvements inside the car designed to ensure the driver's safety in the event of a crash, and other changes to keep the car on the ground in the case of a spinout. There is no one who would argue the need for these improvements, particularly in the wake of Dale Earnhardt Sr.'s death as a result of a crash during the Daytona 500 in February 2001.

However, the sport's leadership went further. In an effort to broaden the fan base of the sport, NASCAR became more directly involved with the actions of the drivers and crew chiefs, such as fining them for using bad language on the radio or for fighting with other drivers. It also tried to regulate bump-drafting—a form of racing in which two drivers literally hook rear bumper to front bumper to push to the front using both speed and aerodynamics. At courses such as Talladega, bump-drafting created exciting racing. Fans loved it, because it inevitably led to some sort of "bump and run" that created winners, and losers, on the track.

NASCAR lost sight of its authentic and actual brand when making these changes that impacted the excitement, emotional resonance, and connectivity of the sport with its fans. Stock car racing was built on big personalities—from Junior Johnson to "King" Richard Petty to Dale Earnhardt Sr. These men and the others who are looked at as the founding fathers of NASCAR had no friends on the oval racetracks, and they were known for settling grudges with a well-placed bump or a well-timed spin. Both Dale Sr. and his son, Dale Earnhardt Jr., the most popular driver in the sport today, were experts at bump-drafting and used it to win races (and sometimes spin out opponents). The grudges were legendary, the fans loyal. Earnhardt's fans were among the most passionate, despite the fact that he was as known for wrecking drivers he couldn't pass as he was for winning.

As the sport sought to curb the personalities of its drivers, among the most fan- and media-available in the world, support for it waned. As a result of the new rules of behavior, it was hard to tell one driver from the other—they became milquetoast (a word you would never use to describe Earnhardt Senior, Junior Johnson, Darrell Waltrip, or any of the old-timers) as a result of the new rules. Innovation may have made drivers safer, but it also made the sport boring to many.

Recognizing this, in late 2009 and for the 2010 season, NASCAR reinvented itself. It introduced the double-file restart after a caution flag, and it decided to "let the drivers be drivers" and to standardize start times across all of its races. The double-file restart added some much-needed excitement back into racing, and it has been popular with fans. The "let the drivers be drivers" motto has not been tested, but it, and the standard start times, seemed to resonate with the fans as well. The sport also removed its rule on bump-drafting, making races like those at Talladega exciting once again. Additionally, NASCAR has changed its schedule for 2011, removing venues such as Atlanta Motor Speedway and adding new sites like Kentucky, and it has further refined and simplified the scoring system to make it easier for fans to follow the competition between drivers.

According to *Street & Smith's SportsBusiness Journal*, "Nobody knows if the various moves will work. The decision to move most of the race start times to 1 p.m. ET, for example, runs counter to every ratings lesson sports media executives have learned over the past 30 years. Since the early 1970s, leagues and networks have figured out that later start times almost always lead to higher ratings. But NASCAR and Fox believe the sport's move to make uniform start times early on a Sunday afternoon will be just what it needs."

"The NASCAR viewer wants to go to church, come back, sit down and watch NASCAR," Fox Sports ad sales chief Neil Mulcahy said. "We tried to make it as uniform as possible. NASCAR is coming off a year in which its TV ratings dropped to their lowest point in a decade and attendance was flat or down at most tracks."

David Hill, chief executive at Fox Sports, has been a longtime proponent of embracing the contact that makes NASCAR a "contact sport" and returning racing back to its roots. "I was very pleased they decided to make the changes," Hill said. "They listened to the fan base, and they are very smart for doing that."[6]

In this case—in fact, in almost every case—reinvention required that the sport look outside itself, to its consumers and paying customers, to see what it could do to reinforce and enhance its core positioning. It looked at simple steps it could take that would make its brand more attractive to its target, yet remain true to its core. And it acted.

NASCAR's return to its core seems to be having a positive impact on the sport. An article on Yahoo! Sports says, "The racing, like it has been for most of the year, was much improved [in 2009 and 2010]. . . . The 'have at it' policy, designed to allow drivers to self-police on the track while also encouraging more emotion . . . gave NASCAR a juicy storyline when teammates Denny Hamlin and Kyle Busch raced each other hard for a shot at the win."[7] Reinvention, starting with going back to its core, seems to be working for some of NASCAR's constituents, though its ratings and attendance remain anemic in the short term and a longer-term effort may be required with differing promotional and advertising initiatives.

However, the leaders of the sport are taking a long-term view as well. When asked the current state of NASCAR, Hall of Fame driver Richard Petty said, "You know it's really hard to say. Are we going to compare it with 10 years ago, five years ago or last year? It could be better. We could have better racing. We could have more fans. We could have more enthusiasm. But we've been through this before, as far as NASCAR, if you'll look back at history. They'll grow real good and then they kind of flatten out and then they'll grow some more. So right now we're in a flat state."[8]

Reinventing a Category

Reinvention also meets undetectable needs with obvious products, and in the course of doing so may reinvent a category. Take the case of Truvia, a natural sweetener made from the stevia plant. A creation of Cargill, Truvia was introduced to an already crowded sweetener marketplace in 2008. With so many other sweeteners on the market—Equal, Sweet'n Low, and Splenda, to name a few—why introduce Truvia?

Simply, at the point of its introduction, Truvia was a no-brainer—or at least as much of a no-brainer as it could be with millions of dollars of investment capital at stake. Today, more than at any time in history, Americans are turning more and more to organic foods untouched by chemicals. They are looking for all-natural foods that will help them lose weight or at least maintain their current weight. Truvia does just that—it's all-natural, and it doesn't add calories.

For Cargill, Truvia is at the heart of its brand. Cargill is a private company that is an international provider and marketer of foods and agricultural products, among other things. It prides itself on its scientific expertise. The creation and marketing of Truvia speaks directly to its brand positioning.

And Cargill's investment paid off. According to Portfolio .com, "In just 15 months, Cargill Inc.'s plant-based Truvia sweetener has grown into an estimated $40 million business for the food and agriculture giant, becoming Cargill's single-biggest U.S. consumer brand. . . . Truvia holds a market lead, according to Nielsen data, and it accounts for 58 percent of retail U.S. sales among stevia sweeteners."[9]

When it comes right down to it, reinvention is about demand—consumer or customer demand—as it relates to brands. It requires a deep understanding of consumer and customer needs and preferences, not simply market research to know what's selling, but research that gets below the surface to understand why.

Latent Demand and Reinvention

Latent demand is particularly observable with productivity-oriented technology tools. Remember the Palm Pilot? (If you don't, take a look at HP's recently announced purchase of Palm as the company searches for a way to reinvent its own wireless phone business.) The Palm Pilot was bulky and expensive—but every businessperson wanted one.

The forerunner to the BlackBerry and iPhone, the Palm Pilot met the need businesspeople had for keeping calendars and notes on the go and in a convenient size. However, Palm missed the boat entirely when it came to business e-mail and Internet access. BlackBerry did not. Though slow to go to color,

BlackBerry, while not the coolest of the PDAs (that, based upon the millions sold since introduction, may be Apple's iPhone or the recently introduced fast-selling line of Android-based smart-phones), is still the go-to brand for businesses and corporate IT departments. That's simply because its renovations do not inter-fere with its basic function: secure business e-mail, delivered promptly.

Notwithstanding this fact, the gap is closing between Research in Motion (RIM—the manufacturer of the BlackBerry) and Apple, and unless BlackBerry undertakes a more aggres-sive reinvention agenda, Apple may make further inroads into BlackBerry market share as more progressive and creatively driven companies migrate their platforms once again to the Mac.

And Palm? Well, it was too little, too late for this brand. Its attempt to join the smartphone market—the Palm Pre—got lost in a sea of competitors and failed to reengage former buy-ers who had shifted their loyalties to these competitors that had clear points of differentiation and distinctiveness, and the company was sold to Hewlett-Packard for $1 billion. Its epitaph, according to the *Wall Street Journal*: "Palm, a onetime mobile device pioneer with its Palm Pilot, has been eclipsed by Apple Inc.'s iPhone, Research In Motion Ltd.'s BlackBerry and devices running Google Inc.'s Android software. The company recently hired bankers to explore a sale amid weak demand for its newest phones, the Pre and Pixi."[10]

REMEMBER

- A brand's core essence is the underpinning for reinvention.
- All reinvention is based on consumer and customer insights.
- Reinvention helps uncover dormant and hidden demands and creates products to meet those needs. (Or, saying it more directly, reinvention can "steal" ideas from consumers to successfully exploit existing behavior for commercial gain.)
- Reinvention can result in sustainable competitive advantages.
- Most important, reinvention creates profits—at considerably lower risk and less expense than a strategy that is solely innovation driven.

Your Reputation Precedes You

**Brand management and the successful reinvention
of a company or enterprise are inextricably linked to
reputation management; if one is at risk, so is the other.**

A company's reputation is the external embodiment and quintessence of its core essence. Put bluntly, that reputation in the marketplace has bottom-line impact. As such, it's a marketing concern: brand marketing is inextricably linked to reputation management. And one bad act or misspoken word—whether unintentional or misinterpreted—can have repercussions with consumers or customers that impact and undermine a brand's core essence, its positioning, and its attributes for years.

Doing "God's Work"

Goldman Sachs is the most recent high-profile case study (among several in 2010) of the consequences of not understanding this critical relationship and connection. Goldman Sachs, the renowned financial institution, had long envisioned itself as the master of the "masters of the universe" that run Wall Street. And then the financial crisis hit, bringing with it extreme populist anger toward Wall Street, and especially toward Goldman, which the media portrayed as seeming to have made money betting on both sides of the market for its own profit at the expense of its clients. And as of this writing, Goldman Sachs is number one on CNN's list of "Most Hateable Companies (Not Named BP)."[1]

In an effort to stem this anger and make its side of the story public, Goldman aggressively reached out to the media. Its first step was to give the *Times* of London access to its chairman, Lloyd Blankfein.[2] This action, headlined "Goldman Sachs PR Blitz," was first on the list of "Dumbest Moments in Business 2009" by CNNMoney.com.[3] (And it was potentially even surpassed in January 2011 by Goldman's embarrassing rescission and change of heart regarding the opportunity for its prized wealthiest U.S. clients, including corporate heads and board members of the nation's largest companies, to invest in Facebook because of worries that the deal would run afoul of securities regulators.)

Goldman's publicity blitz received that "accolade" for good reason: the company apparently started this public relations campaign without thinking about the key messages it wanted to convey. In fact, it seemed to assume somewhat arrogantly that its reputation would restore itself once access was granted. As a result, Goldman Sachs damaged its brand—at least in the short or medium term.

How? In the excerpts from the disastrous interview that follow, pay attention to how John Aldridge, staff writer for the *Times*, can barely contain his incredulity as Mr. Blankfein speaks words that will live for years in histories written about the Great Recession:

> "We're very important," he (Blankfein) says, abandoning self-flagellation. "We help companies to grow by helping them to raise capital. Companies that grow create wealth. This, in turn, allows people to have jobs that create more growth and more wealth. It's a virtuous cycle." To drive home his point, he makes a remarkably bold claim. "We have a social purpose."
>
> "Everybody should be, frankly, happy," he says. Can he be serious? Deadly. Goldman's performance, he argues, is the firmest indication of a nascent economic recovery that will benefit not just him and his firm but all of us. "The financial system led us into the crisis and it will lead us out."
>
> Blankfein goes on to say something equally audacious. We should welcome the return of titanic paydays at Goldman . . .
>
> He is, he says, just a banker "doing God's work."[4]

Blankfein remains oblivious to the impact his words have on Goldman's reputation. On December 17, 2010, *The New York Daily News* reported he was overheard bragging about the price of a piece of art in his office, refocusing media scrutiny on his bank. His words brought the spotlight back to Goldman as its executives were set to receive record bonuses totaling more than $100 million, reigniting lingering anger at those who many believe were the instigators of the continuing recession that has unemployment hovering at 9 percent.[5]

Mr. Blankfein very simply and desperately needed proper and nuanced message points because the perception of what he said was met with the reality of what people were experiencing. His saying, "We help companies to grow by helping them to raise capital" underscored for many the fact and reality that they could not raise capital or get loans—credit markets were frozen as a result of perceived actions that Goldman and other big banks (they were now banks, as a result of taking federal money) took. As a result, no jobs were created—in fact, more than 10 million people were unemployed at the time of his ill-conceived comments, many having lost their jobs as a result of this credit freeze. Companies went under, millions lost their jobs and their homes—and Mr. Blankfein insisted people should be happy.

CNNMoney.com perhaps said it best, in reference to this interview. "For all the complex financial products they can dream up, simple common sense still seems to elude the bright minds of Wall Street. Or at least, Goldman Sachs CEO Lloyd Blankfein."[6]

There is no better recent example of the value of creating consistency in messaging, sharing this consistency across the company, from the CEO to the night janitor, and preparing for an adversarial opponent than this well-intended but unfortunate interview. The creation of key messages and talking points (and internalizing a script so that the delivery of key points is both natural and believable) could have helped enhance Goldman's brand; instead, this seemingly off-the-cuff conversation fed the anger of those Americans who—rightly or wrongly—blamed the bankers for high unemployment and for the foreclosure mess. They, in turn, riled up their representatives in Congress, who become emboldened and determined to implement more financial regulation.

Competence Would Have Led to Less Damage

In Goldman's case, company leaders may have known the potential communications issues the company faced, but from the outside they didn't seem to care, or, even worse, were less than competent to manage. They seemed to think they were speaking into an echo chamber, where Goldman's institutional brilliance and magnificence would be reflected back at it; instead the company faced populist scorn, and even more damage to its brand. Goldman has not yet recovered from this blow, and it is at risk of continuing to be characterized as a firm with a lack of humility bordering on haughtiness. As of this writing it's still clear that, when Goldman does speak, it remains on the defensive.

Since a company's reputation is so precious to its brand, marketing must always be prepared to defend it, especially if—or when—a company is under regulatory scrutiny. On April 16, 2010, the Securities and Exchange Commission accused Goldman of fraud relating to its action in the mortgage markets. Goldman was accused of playing both sides of the street, allegedly creating and selling a "mortgage investment that was secretly devised to fail."[7] Goldman was caught flat-footed, and in a response clearly crafted by the legal department it called the commission's accusations "completely unfounded in law and fact" and said it would "vigorously contest them and defend the firm and its reputation."[8] However, the company let too much time go by without responding, either off the record or on, and defending its brand in language that resonated with Main Street.

The trickle of bad news became a rush when e-mails that the bank had turned over to a Senate subcommittee were made public. Now, understand, when Goldman turned these e-mails over to the subcommittee, company leaders knew there was a chance the messages would be made public—and yet, when they were, the bank was again unprepared to respond in any real or meaningful way.

The e-mails were, from a communications standpoint, damaging. According to Forbes.com, "Goldman, theoretically, is innocent until proven guilty. However, in the public eye, the firm has also become the poster child for Wall Street greed and excess."[9] The e-mails seemed to make a liar out of Goldman's executives. According to the *Washington Post*:

> The documents show that the firm's executives were celebrating earlier investments calculated to benefit if housing prices fell. . . . In an e-mail sent in the fall of 2007, for example, Goldman executive Donald Mullen predicted a windfall because credit-rating companies had downgraded mortgage-related investments, which caused losses for investors.
>
> "Sounds like we will make some serious money," Mullen wrote.[10]

Even worse for Goldman, the e-mails boasted about taking advantage of those who could least afford it. Referring to the U.S. subprime mortgage market, one e-mail labels borrowers as "not too brilliant," and notes that the "poor little subprime borrowers will not last too long!!!" Other e-mails were dismissive of the derivative-based financial products that Goldman was making a killing on, comparing their very existence to something "like Frankenstein['s monster]," noting that what they were selling (ABS CDO^2—asset-backed collateralized debt obligations squared) was something that "has no purpose, which is absolutely conceptual and highly theoretical and which nobody knows how to price."[11] Eventually, as we all know by now, Frankenstein's monster turned on its creator, leaving much destruction in its wake.

The Impact

The impact of this trickle of hubris followed by a torrent of ego was immediate—a badly tarnished reputation, which cannot be reinvented (but possibly can be restored), as well as a lowered stock price (down nearly 10 percent on May 1, 2010, in the wake of more bad news about criminal charges).[12] Simon Johnson, a former International Monetary Fund economist who is now a finance professor at the Massachusetts Institute of Technology's Sloan School of Management, sums up the aftermath: "Clearly, they've become a toxic asset."[13]

Toxic. Never would anyone on Wall Street think that word would be associated with Goldman Sachs. All because it allowed journalists and correspondents to render a portrait in words that it had sacrificed its brand to the egos of the investment bankers and traders. Goldman Sachs leaders believed their own press that Goldman's investment bankers and traders were the best, and that no one—not the media, the government, or Main Street—could hurt the company. They were wrong.

Much of this maelstrom could have been avoided if Goldman Sachs had had an actionable and effective communications plan in place to protect the sanctity of the brand. At the beginning of the Great Recession, as layoffs continued and homes were lost and as banks were bailed out and individual Americans weren't, the anger against Wall Street was growing palpable—and it was real. There was no sense that Wall Street, which controlled the credit markets, was sharing the pain, or even understood that others were feeling pain. As the layoffs and loss of homes continued, news came of large bonuses on Wall Street—amounts of money that most people couldn't even imagine—for doing what, exactly?

Managing the Brand—Maintaining the Company's Reputation

What should Goldman have done? The company's leaders should have recognized the growing concern and outright resentment outside the company's walls and prepared a marketing and communications reinvention strategy that positioned Goldman Sachs as a strong proponent of necessary financial reforms while preparing a defense of its brand.

There's no escaping the fact that Goldman leaders knew the company was being investigated by regulators and the government. It seems, however, that they believed that they would skate through thanks to Goldman's influence and standing. They did not prepare a strategy that dealt with the worst-case scenario.

This kind of nuanced and complex scenario planning is imperative in reputation management. Communicators should assume the best, yet prepare for the worst—especially when regulators are involved. And never, ever, assume that the company's influence is greater than that of Main Street—especially in an election year. The main reason for this type of care is summed up by Felix Salmon in the *Washington Post*:

> On the Friday that the SEC charges were announced, and again on the following Sunday, Blankfein left voicemail messages for all the firm's employees, saying, in his characteristically combative way, that Goldman would fight the charges.
>
> But those weren't the calls that really mattered. The truly important conversations were taking place in the boardrooms of Goldman's clients, and between those clients and bankers at rival shops. Have you read the complaint? they asked—and the answer was always yes. And do you still trust Goldman Sachs? The answer to that was no. . . . Without its clients' trust, the Goldman franchise crumbles, and the bank becomes just an ordinary trading shop. No longer can it charge a premium for its mergers and acquisitions advisory services, or its stock and bond underwriting, or its customized structured products. To put it in baseball terms, it has lost what another storied franchise, the Yankees, so closely guards—its mystique and aura.[14]

In July 2010, Goldman Sachs settled the SEC suit for $550 million. But questions linger about the long-term damage to its reputation.

REMEMBER

- Pay extremely close attention to the sentiment being expressed in blogs or online—they are often a precursor for what is to come, and they may influence the cable news cycle.
- Prepare strong, simple, clear messaging about the brand that is repeated constantly through many different internal and external channels.
- Never let an executive or representative speak to a reporter without preparation or without talking points that have been thoroughly and repeatedly reviewed and practiced.
- Assume the best, but prepare for the worst. Have internal and external communications available that can immediately be sent to employees and constituents if the company or the brand finds itself in a difficult predicament.
- Give key players across the company talking points to use with clients and employees.
- Never, ever assume a company's reputation will get it through any difficulty.

Play Nicely Together . . . or Else

Maintaining a brand's core essence in the face of public relations crises is essential and of great consequence. The relationship between marketing and public relations must be reinvented in a way that protects the core because how a company or enterprise communicates does matter.

Toyota, Goldman Sachs, Johnson & Johnson, BP, HP. Between 2009 and 2010, each of these companies faced public relations concerns that ultimately escalated into crises. In most of these situations, the brand was damaged, and in one of these occurrences, old issues were revived that brought an ugly past back into the spotlight. In almost every instance, crisis managers from respected public relations firms were retained and brought in, congressional hearings were televised to an engaged public, and reputations suffered. And once the company's reputation was damaged, the brand was likewise damaged—if not for the long term, certainly for the foreseeable future.

Public Relations and Marketing

When a crisis strikes, most chief executives and boards look outside the company or enterprise for "experts" to help them navigate the shoals upon which corporate reputations can be shredded and torn asunder. At KPMG, when the firm went through a very serious matter and accusations by the U.S. Department of Justice regarding allegedly illegal U.S. tax shelters, the leadership team turned to a score of crisis management experts—individuals with connections to then current Bush administration—to help steer the firm through the regulatory labyrinth. Among the experts brought in were several attorneys with expertise in dealing with the Department of Justice and a boutique communications firm that specialized in media-oriented crisis communications.

All of these experts were brought in for leadership, by leadership, and their presence was a comfort to all . . . leaders. But in the case of communications, the actual work was done by KPMG's integrated and combined marketing and communications team, working directly with the chairman and the board.

Why? The KPMG brand, the KPMG workforce, and KPMG clients were directly impacted and influenced by the preponderance of daily rumor and innuendo in a period of uncertainty, and no one knew how to communicate with these internal and external audience segments as well as the KPMG marketing and communications managers and directors, particularly our head of corporate communications, George Ledwith, who astutely managed our public relations every day.

These brand-focused individuals were uniquely positioned to create the messages that would persuasively resonate with our key constituents. However, they often faced an uphill battle that is not uncommon in corporate America. As Peter Goodman of the *New York Times* corroborates, "In times of crisis, communications professionals and lawyers often pursue conflicting agendas. Communications strategists are inclined to mollify public anger with expressions of concern, while lawyers warn that contrition can be construed as admissions of guilt in potentially expensive lawsuits."[1] That battle is fought every day, in every corporation—at least in my experience—and it is one lawyers often win, as the natural propensity of leadership is to financially protect the company.

Critically, marketing has only one agenda—protecting the brand. And the success of KPMG's marketing and communications professionals' efforts, working collaboratively with the office of the general counsel, resulted in the loss of less than a handful of clients during what was a very dark and threatening period.

Damaging the Core: Toyota's Troubles

The time from the beginning of the recession (late 2008) through the conception and formation of this book (early 2011) has been a particularly painful and difficult time for many businesses' and enterprises' reputations. Lehman Brothers imploded and disappeared; Fannie Mae and Freddie Mac, once the hope of many homeowners, became pariahs; and Goldman Sachs, BP, and Toyota seem to have lost their places in the pantheon of great brands.

In the case of Toyota, it strayed from its essence by doing something anathema to its brand—taking an adversarial position with its customers, who are often not only brand loyalists but also the company's best brand ambassadors. That the company took a defensive position is not surprising—the first response of any person or company when the core of their existence is under fire is to fight. But in the case of Toyota, essential to the brand's core was the company's reputation for putting the consumer first. That is why Toyota's position when the initial media reports of issues with its cars' accelerators first came to light was such a shock. The company's reaction went against almost all that its brand stood for to its buyers. And the corporation suffered for it.

Some may see this as an overreaction—Toyota isn't the first company to recall cars, and it won't be the last. But at the core of Toyota's brand is its relationship with its customers, who were loyal to the point of mania. And that may be impaired, if not ruined.

For an automaker—in fact, for all but a few brands—reputation is everything. That's why the automaker finally admitted mistakes, apologized, and accepted a fine from the U.S. government. It has tried to move on, and in response to the crisis, rolled out new advertising that has focused on Toyota buyers' continuing loyalty. But appealing to those who already own Toyotas won't help the car company's share price recover. It needs to appeal to those consumers who might have bought a Toyota in the past, but are now afraid to because of perceived safety issues. Those three words—*perceived safety issues*—are anathema to automakers, so it is not surprising that Toyota has a long way to go. As a first step to restoring its brand reputation, securing its base is an interesting strategy, but the more provocative story is yet to be written.

BP and the Age of Twitter

Responsible for the worst oil spill in history: that is how BP will be described in reports and conversation for many years to come. That's an extremely difficult position for a company that previously saw itself as an exemplar of corporate social responsibility and branded itself as being a part of the alternative energy solution, beyond petroleum.

When the oil rig explosion and resulting oil spill in the Gulf of Mexico occurred, BP mishandled about every step of its communications. According to Howard Rubenstein, a well-known and well-regarded public relations strategist, "It was one of the worst P.R. approaches that I've seen in my 56 years of business. . . . They tried to be opaque. They had every excuse in the book. Right away they should have accepted responsibility and recognized what a disaster they faced. They basically thought they could spin their way out of catastrophe. It doesn't work that way."[2]

Originally, the chief spokesman for the company was its chief executive officer, Tony Hayward. However, every time he opened his mouth, he appeared to misspeak. Peter Goldman reported in the *New York Times*, "When [Hayward] apologized to those harmed by the spill . . . he tacked on two sentences that would overshadow all else. 'There's no one who wants this thing over more than I do,' he said. 'I'd like my life back.' . . . With this, Mr. Hayward opened the gates to Sound-Bite Hell."[3]

While the company was experiencing the ensuing difficulties of the 24-hour news cycle, which constantly replayed that video, it was also being impacted by new media, specifically Twitter, where a fake account, @BPGlobalPR, snarkily made fun of the company's response to the disaster. The *Public Relations Strategist*, a publication of the Public Relations Society of America, followed the fake campaign: "At 3:07 p.m. on May 19—29 days after the start of the Gulf oil crisis—@BPGlobalPR sent out its first tweet: 'We regretfully admit that something has happened off of the Gulf Coast. More to come.'"[4]

Prior to the Gulf oil spill—prior to this parody account—BP had no presence on Twitter. BP leaders had overlooked the importance of social media in getting out or responding to news, and they didn't understand the conversations that resulted from the posting of the news. If marketing had been involved from the beginning, perhaps this important channel would not have been overlooked. Instead, company leaders had another fire they had to put out. The *Public Relations Strategist* article reports,

> BP spokespeople have acknowledged the account and apparently contacted Twitter to make @BPGlobalPR clearly label itself as a parody. The inquiry led to a change in @BPGlobalPR's bio, which temporarily read: "We are not associated with Beyond Petroleum, the company that has been destroying the Gulf of Mexico for 50 days. . . . For the most part, BP officials have ignored @BPGlobalPR, which might be all they can do."[5]

In the same article, *Public Relations Strategist* went on to enumerate three lessons to be learned from this disaster as it relates to Twitter, and they are lessons marketers should already know:

>> Communication doesn't matter as much as action.
>> How you communicate matters.
>> Learn social media before a crisis occurs.[6]

An Ugly Divorce, Corporate Style

Hewlett Packard is no stranger to boardroom intrigue that causes increased public scrutiny. In 2005 it fired its then chairman and

CEO, Carly Fiorina. The immediate cause was the perceived failure of the acquisition of Compaq, which Fiorina had led, and which engendered a proxy fight with one of the Hewlett family heirs. Shortly after that, interim chairwoman Patricia Dunn and the HP board got embroiled in a spying scandal the likes of which was previously unheard of in the corporate world.

In that case, HP admitted to spying on its own board of directors to find out who was leaking information to the press. It did so by using private investigators to pose as the directors and call phone companies seeking the directors' phone records. Dunn was accused of orchestrating this "investigation" and of trying to keep it a secret. As a result of this scandal, Dunn left the company and Mark Hurd was named chairman and CEO. HP's focus turned to cost cutting and to creating a culture in which the Compaq-HP merger could become profitable for the company. Mr. Hurd was seen to be a good leader, at least before the Great Recession made things difficult for all businesses. A Bloomberg article noted of Hurd, "He's well regarded by Wall Street for turning the company from a bureaucratic has-been to a market leader again. In the first 2½ years of Hurd's tenure as leader, H-P's stock increased 137 percent. For the last two years, however, H-P's stock performance has been mediocre, dropping 5 percent. Although that was better than the NASDAQ, it tracked that index very closely over that period."[7]

The HP board, once again in the thick of the issues, fired Hurd in the summer of 2010 amid allegations of ethical shortcomings. It was leaked that he had a "personal relationship" with a contractor hired by the company.[8] Although shocking to Wall Street, Hurd's "resignation" and separation from the company seemed on the surface amicable. No allegations were made that Hurd had had an inappropriate sexual relationship with the contractor—in fact, the board went out of its way to say that there was no sexual harassment, as did the woman's attorney. Rather, it was the misuse of his expense account that was given as the official reason for Mr. Hurd's resignation.

Then things moved beyond the internal confines of HP. Larry Ellison, cofounder and chief executive officer of Oracle Corporation, poured scorn on the HP board's decision to let Mr.

Hurd go. In an e-mail to the *New York Times*, Ellison lambasted the HP board. He wrote, "The HP board just made the worst personnel decision since the idiots on the Apple board fired Steve Jobs many years ago. . . . That decision nearly destroyed Apple and would have if Steve hadn't come back and saved them. . . . In losing Mark Hurd, the HP board failed to act in the best interest of HP's employees, shareholders, customers and partners. . . . The HP board admits that it fully investigated the sexual harassment claims against Mark and found them to be utterly false."[9]

Mr. Ellison named Mr. Hurd a co-president—and his seeming successor—at Oracle within a month of his dismissal from Hewlett-Packard. The *Times* picked up on this and remarked that "In naming Mark V. Hurd, the former chief executive of Hewlett-Packard, as Oracle's new co-president, Lawrence J. Ellison, Oracle's chief executive and largest shareholder, has put his money where his controversial mouth is."[10]

It might have ended there, but HP's board, as in the spying scandal, did not know when to let go. It sued Oracle, with whom it partners on some ventures, as well as Hurd, and as a result, continued to receive unflattering media coverage, including this from the *New York Times*:

> Hewlett-Packard's tumultuous breakup with its former chief executive Mark V. Hurd may soon warrant its own reality TV show. The latest installment arrived on Tuesday, as HP filed a lawsuit in the Superior Court of California in Santa Clara against Mr. Hurd. The suit accused Mr. Hurd of violating his severance agreement to protect HP's confidential information by taking a job as co-president of Oracle, an HP rival and partner. . . . "In his new positions, Hurd will be in a situation in which he cannot perform his duties for Oracle without necessarily using and disclosing HP's trade secrets and confidential information to others," HP said in its lawsuit.[11]

The suit was settled within a month, with Hurd agreeing to give up about half of the severance owed him.

In the case of HP, it seems that most of its public relations disasters were created internally, from the firing of Fiorina, to the spying scandal, to the firing of Hurd, to the suit against Oracle. These are not marketing missteps, but rather strategic or leadership errors and blunders. The board seemed consumed (and properly so) with risk, but not with the risk its decisions and actions, however well intended, unnecessarily placed on the HP brand. The continued absence of a considered perspective on reputation and brand impact has shown that HP's board is short-sighted and ill prepared for today's global, 24/7 Internet-driven news cycle and environment. Interestingly, in early 2011, the HP board once again reopened the Hurd matter when, as a result of shareholder lawsuits, the new members of the board initiated an independent probe of Hurd and the circumstances surrounding his separation agreement. Not so surprisingly, four of the directors involved in the decision to oust Hurd said they wouldn't stand for reelection and the company named five new directors to take their places.

REMEMBER

- Marketing must participate in the management of a crisis and lead the reinvention of the brand following a calamity, emergency, or disaster. It must have a seat at the table when a crisis hits because it holds intimate knowledge of the key audiences, including the most important audience, customers and consumers.
- Marketing itself must also reinvent how it responds after a crisis. This is where understanding the core is fundamental. If the brand has been harmed, a company must return to the actions and activities that made it great. Key to that is its connection to brand loyalists.
- Public relations and marketing must reinvent their sometimes adversarial relationship. In each case, the customer and consumer are the focus of the messaging. Together, the teams may be able to craft a response to a crisis that mitigates the damage to a brand's core.

Sleep Soundly, Work Fearfully

The first 10 years of the 21st century have demonstrated to all Americans that life can change radically, often in a matter of minutes. As a marketer, be prepared for the unexpected and have reinvention plans already in place that will work in any situation.

W hile a brand's core essence is unchanging, it can be impacted by events beyond anyone's control—events that seemingly happen in the blink of an eye, like an explosion on an oil rig. Living with this reality is something Americans have become increasingly familiar with in the 21st century. It began with fears of Y2K—all of our computers were going to crash at the dawning of the new century, and instantaneously, all data would be lost. It was then that we for the first time truly realized what a computer-dependent world this was. Businesses invested millions of dollars in preparing for Y2K— and the century turned quietly. No data (or nothing more than the most minuscule of bits and bytes) was lost.

Then, in 2001, there was 9/11. This engendered fear unlike any experience since, perhaps, World War II and the bombing at Pearl Harbor. While the United States had experienced "homegrown" terrorism in the form of Timothy McVeigh and the Unabomber, it had not dealt with an adversary that wanted to—and did—kill Americans simply for being American. On that fateful day, more than 3,000 people lost their lives, and all Americans lost their sense of security. Everything changed in a matter of moments on a beautiful early fall day. Shortly thereafter, the country was at war in Afghanistan and Iraq—as it would be almost a decade later. Yet the fear of the unknown terrorist is real and continuing, as was seen in the thwarted airplane bombing at Christmas 2009 and the attempted bombing in Times Square in New York in 2010.

In 2008, there was the Great Recession. The American Dream was always the home with the white picket fence, a good job, and enough money to retire on. In one fell swoop, it seemed, the Great Recession took all of that away—the mortgage crisis led to record numbers of foreclosures in which countless people lost their homes, and the stock market dropped by more than 42 percent, initially taking with it many people's retirement savings. As a result of a freeze in the credit markets, businesses drastically downsized or even closed and Americans were out of work in record numbers. No home, no job, and no savings—it doesn't get much scarier than that "perfect storm" scenario. All sense of traditional and widely accepted types of security were gone. The American psyche took a tremendous blow, and its repercussions, in all likelihood, will continue for decades to come. Understanding this massive jolt and the impact it will have on customer loyalty or consumer buying patterns is the job of the marketer. And while the government's numbers show that the Great Recession ended in 2009, for Americans, the impact of that economically troubled time continues.

The Great Recession's Impact

According to the *McKinsey Quarterly*, "This much is certain: when we finally enter into the post-crisis period, the business and economic context will not have returned to its pre-crisis state. Executives preparing their organizations to succeed in the new normal must focus on what has changed and what remains basically the same for their customers, companies, and industries. The result will be an environment that, while different from the past, is no less rich in possibilities for those who are prepared."[1]

American businesses experienced the recession differently than the American public. Always somewhat risk averse, companies now are even more so. They have retreated into a comfort zone where smaller is better, and cash is more often than not king. This is not a bad thing by a long stretch, but it does dramatically impact marketing.

In this scenario, it would seem that marketing, which should have its finger on the pulse of the consumer or customer, would lead the rush to reinvention. In fact, the reaction of marketers was slow to come and lacked an understanding of the broad changes that happened in such a short time to the American landscape. Almost overnight, it seems, Americans returned to a 1950s way of life with a 21st century twist.

Reinventing an Automotive Company

One company that "got it" quickly was Ford Motor Company. Having established a strong cash position earlier in the decade, it was the only one of the Big Three not to take any federal bailout money. As a result, it escaped the federal oversight—including televised congressional hearings guaranteed to make almost any CEO look bad—and, it seems, the consumer anger that its two brethren in the automotive industry experienced.

Ford did this by reinventing itself in the decade before the recession by selling or shutting down troubled or underperforming brands and returning to its core—making better cars. In fact, in 2010 the Ford Fusion was named *Car and Driver* magazine's Car of the Year—a huge honor in the industry. Recalling Ford's resurgence, executive chairman Bill Ford Jr. told the Associated Press, "Even when we got into tough times, we kept our R&D spending alive, and it was something that I was personally involved in to make sure we spent in the new technologies that will get us to real modernization."[2]

Reinvention Needed—but Missed

Unlike Ford, Dell has resisted the opportunity to successfully reinvent itself—albeit for an effort to follow competitors into the services business and the more recent attempt to expand its Web-based computing services through the acquisition of the software company Boomi. For many years, it was the largest seller of PCs in the United States. It operates to this day, for the most part, on a direct-to-business or direct-to-consumer model—where a customer can have Dell build a computer to the customer's specific requirements. Dell also sold its computers through select retailers. In February 2005 Dell appeared in first place in a ranking of the "Most Admired Companies" published by *Fortune* magazine.

Almost overnight, however, Dell went from first to worst. "Gripes about tech support are on the rise, and the PC king is scrambling to upgrade"[3] a *BusinessWeek* article stated. The article cited a University of Michigan customer satisfaction survey in which Dell's rating fell 6.3 percent from the previous year, as complaints to the Better Business Bureau (which had already risen 23 percent in 2004) rose another 5 percent. A onetime customer favorite was now nothing more than average. "We've never seen a drop like this," says Professor Claes Fornell, who ran the UM survey.[4]

The decline in customer service created a 21st century backlash, as communities of frustrated consumers popped up online (including an ihatedell.net website), with blogs serving to archive and distribute individual complaints to the masses. *BusinessWeek* captured one example perfectly in an article chronicling the company's descent, as it relayed the story of Helaina Burton, who spent three hours on the phone trying to have her faulty keyboard addressed. A half-dozen Dell reps later, her published reaction was that she "certainly won't buy another product from Dell." She went on to promise that she would "make sure that any other prospective Dell customer I meet knows what kind of treatment they'll get."[5]

The impact was immediate—and directly felt on the bottom line. In November 2005, *BusinessWeek* published an article titled "It's Bad to Worse at Dell"[6] about shortfalls in projected earnings and sales, with a worse-than-predicted third-quarter financial performance—a bad omen for a company that had routinely underestimated its earnings. On January 31, 2007, Kevin B. Rollins, CEO of the company since 2004, resigned as both CEO and as a director, and Michael Dell resumed his former role as CEO. Investors and many shareholders had called for Rollins's resignation because of poor company performance. At the same time, the company announced that, for the fourth time in five quarters, earnings would fail to reach consensus analyst estimates.

Perhaps nothing crystallizes Dell's issues better than faulty computers it sold to businesses and individuals alike. From 2003 to 2005 Dell sold millions of PCs that leaked chemicals and malfunctioned in other manners—and when it got complaints, blamed the users for overtaxing the machines. This fact only came to light when a lawsuit against the company became public in mid-2010.

Reporting on the lawsuit, the *New York Times* produced a damning account of the company that showed millions of Dell computers that had been sold to major companies across the spectrum were "leaking chemicals and causing the malfunctions." The article went on to reveal that Dell employees were aware that their products were likely to break and downplayed the issue to affected customers. According to the *Times*, the issue was so pervasive that "even the firm defending Dell in the lawsuit was affected when Dell balked at fixing 1,000 suspect computers, according to e-mail messages revealed in the dispute."[7]

Dell has been off track all this time for a very simple reason: it has lost sight of its core, which was more than an efficient manufacturing and pricing model—it was an emotional connection with its customers, who felt its customer service was top-notch. It did not recognize the marketplace was changing all too quickly: businesses were reducing their technology expenditures, and consumers (and non-U.S. markets) were the growing opportunity—one Dell started to treat with less respect just as the market changed. Dell remains a company in search of a new identity—and a brand that is out of touch with its core essence. Until it revisits that essence, it cannot and will not successfully reinvent itself.

The New Vacation

As a result of this "one day you're up, and the next day you're down" mentality, corporations have hunkered down. They are working fearfully—not reinventing, but going back to the well-known, comforting, and familiar.

This, more than at any other time in recent memory, is a time when companies should be studying their core essence to better understand their relationship with the consumer or customer. And marketers should be researching their brands to see what aspects of their products and services resonate with their buyers and targets—and why.

One hard-hit industry in the downturn was travel and leisure. As a result of curtailing spending, consumers reinvented how they take vacation breaks. Now, instead of lengthy and exotic holidays, they take:

>> Staycations (stay at home during their few days off)
>> Daycations (one- to three-day car trips instead of longer visits)
>> Negations (just don't take a vacation)

As time goes on, it has become clear that the two most important factors in how Americans spend time off today are value and shorter durations and distances. Very simply, the U.S. consumer has shifted away from lavish vacations to more value-oriented offerings and closer-to-home attractions. In fact, the industry has faced vacation spending retreating to 1980 levels. This downward trend continues to hurt almost all lodging, casinos, and cruise lines.

This has a direct impact on how leisure and travel is marketed—something marketers are just beginning to realize. If consumers are going on vacation, they want a very good deal. In fact, they want a lower price than they paid last year and an amenity thrown in—at every price point. As a result of the reaction of the industry, some consumers are so confident that they can get a deal that they are negotiating directly with hotels after arrival. This "deal orientation" is both negative and positive for marketers. By reacting in order to fill space, hotels have impacted the perception of their price-value. Consumers now realize that they don't need to spend $500 for a four-star hotel— there are bargains to be had if they only negotiate.

Consumers have reinvented vacationing; now, marketers must reinvent the travel industry. It will take a great strategy and leadership.

REMEMBER

- Revisit the brand's core essence to determine if reinvention is necessary.
- Be prepared for rapid changes by ensuring the brand's messaging is consistent and the brand is true to its positioning.
- Recognize that consumers and customers have fundamentally changed—and reinvent products and services to meet those changes.
- Know that everything can change in moments—and be prepared to carry on.

RULE TWO

YOU HAVE NOTHING WITHOUT THE FOUNDATION

ESSENTIAL TO any reinvention effort is the creation of a strong foundation for a brand. By creating a strong underpinning a brand can be successfully reinvented, but it is a complex, nuanced, and critical undertaking that must include the elements of brand architecture that serve as an external facing navigation tool for customers; the distillation of the core essence in all elements of brand identity; an in-depth understanding of the brand attributes that define a brand's personality; an optimal positioning that drives penetration, preference, and price-value; a brand portfolio strategy that maximizes market coverage and minimizes brand overlap; and a clear and concise understanding of brand equity and the advantages over all other brands.

If the base is not strong—if marketing is creating a product or service line extension that is not valid or authentic to the core essence of the brand—the brand will be suboptimized and the brand's relationship with its loyalists can be damaged.

Strong foundations breed strong brands, and weak foundations create brand disasters.

Integrity Is Next to Godliness

**Brand architecture provides the framework upon which
your brand positioning is built and reinvented.**

T he analogy of a house to describe and discuss the context
of brand architecture, brand attributes, and positioning is
used throughout this book. Importantly, brand architecture
is very similar to the architecture of homes and buildings—it
provides the structural integrity for a brand.

Without a strong foundation, a brand will collapse, just like a
house built on sand does. Attentiveness, conscious design, and
"neatness" (an analogy stand-in description for brand architecture) count here—one misstep, one misaligned room or stairway,
and the structural integrity of a brand can be compromised.

Brand Architecture

According to the *Journal of Brand Management*, "Brand
architecture may be defined as an integrated process of brand
building through establishing brand relationships among
branding options in the competitive environment."[1] The brand
architecture of an organization or company's products or services is in large measure a legacy of past management decisions
as well as the competitive realities the company or enterprise
faces in the marketplace.

Simply stated, brand architecture is how a brand portfolio
relates within the company or enterprise and in the marketplace.
Brand architecture is driven, in part, by how the marketing and

management teams position the brand, combined with the pressures of the market. This is important because positioning drives penetration, preference, and price-value.

Much like the architecture of a home, brand architecture can be thought of as a schematic diagram that identifies the individual elements of the brand so that each component is identified and its contribution to the total brand's appeal and success can be understood. The brand architecture then helps create the brand positioning, which clearly and concisely articulates how customers or consumers should think, feel, and act about the brand. Internally, the brand architecture facilitates an understanding of the brand for everyone in the organization. For each brand manager, or, for that matter, business leader, the architecture provides a clear roadmap of where a brand fits in the overall strategy.

Brand Portfolio Versus Brand Architecture

The terms *brand portfolio* and *brand architecture* are not interchangeable. According to Prophet, a strategic brand and marketing consultancy:

> The two terms are often misunderstood and so clarification can often help demystify the meaning and importance of each concept. Brand portfolio strategy aims to maximize market coverage and minimize brand overlap through the effective creation, deployment, and management of multiple brands within a company. It serves as an inward-facing tool for the organization to ensure that the company's brands are effectively targeting all key segments within the marketplace, working together to maximize sales rather than competing against one another for customers' attention.
>
> In contrast, brand architecture serves as an outward facing navigation tool for customers. It helps minimize customer confusion by laying out the product structure in a way that makes it easy for customers to find what they are looking for and to understand what the company has to offer.[2]

Elements of a Brand's Architecture

Leaders and marketers need to fully and completely understand the emotional benefits, functional benefits, product attributes, occasion appropriateness, and user imagery of the product or service to create the architecture for a brand. It is imperative that marketing and the company or enterprise as a whole share an understanding of the architecture, as well as how it is created.

It begins with the brand attribute or characteristic, which is defined as an objective, tangible feature of the brand. Simply, this means defining why this brand is important to the consumer or customer being targeted. This is a key stage of reinvention, as it can tell you if you have correctly identified your product or service's core essence.

Inevitably, this will lead to a discussion of the benefits that result from using the brand. Benefits are both functional—tangible, noticeable results or outcomes, like time-saving or easy-to-use—and emotional—a psychological impact, like how it makes someone feel good or virtuous for using it (for example, using a "green" cleaning product). The next step is to categorize the benefits into groupings that have common characteristics. These can be tightly or loosely defined.

Once the functional and emotional benefits of the product or service are understood, the key drivers can then be determined—the attributes or benefits that influence the overall decision to purchase or use a product or service. To do this, you need to look at the competition and define what the drivers are within your competitive frame of reference. Key drivers should include the functional and emotional benefits that are revealed by the stated versus derived research (explained in Principle #10).

Cost of Entry

The next step in creating the house your brand "lives in" is looking at the cost of entry-level benefits. These are the drivers that a brand must deliver to be considered a viable alternative to those brands already in the marketplace. In particular, marketers are looking for open opportunities for their brand—drivers for which no brand holds a meaningful competitive edge or advantage. These types of opportunities include, but are not limited to, the high ground not yet taken, as well as benefits that the brand can deliver differently or better than another brand.

Then, brand equity, defined as those drivers where a brand has advantages over all other brands, must be studied and understood. Brand equity includes such things as a brand's associations, brand awareness (aided and unaided), perceived quality, and brand loyalty.

The Three Models of Brand Architecture

When thinking about brand architecture, marketers sometimes believe that it is easier for consumer product companies than service companies. This is not true. During my time at KPMG, we created a brand architecture for this global Big Four accounting, tax, and consulting firm that provided professional services in 146 countries that streamlined and simplified the firm's services globally.

Research showed that the firm's global service lines had separate, but common, brand attributes across disparate cultures and many languages. By determining these attributes, the firm was able to create an overarching and globally agreed positioning as well as separate but complementary positioning for its three service lines. In doing so, the firm was also able to create an overarching or firm-wide positioning: clarity. This modified positioning anticipated the calls in the United States for greater transparency the accounting industry underwent as a result of the systemic failures at Enron and WorldCom and the demise of a competitor—Andersen—as well as the ensuing financial reporting and economic disruptions in the United States, Europe, Asia, and all but a few emerging markets.

Procter & Gamble (P&G) is considered by many to be the ultimate in brand architecture management. Many world-class marketers start their career with this powerhouse consumer packaged goods (CPG) company that has hundreds of brands.

"P&G brand architecture effectively manages the relationship between product, brand and market segments."[3] In this "product brand architecture," the company supports many different product brands with each having its own name and style of expression while the company itself remains invisible to consumers. How many people realize that Wella, Pantene, and Fekkai hair products are P&G brands?

There is also "endorsed brand architecture," in which a "mother" brand is tied to product brands, such as Ford Motor Company (company brand name) and the Taurus automobile (product brand name). Endorsed brands benefit from the standing of their parent and thus may require less up-front investment because consumers see the linkage and there is an assumption of a corporate "halo" around the brand.

The third model of brand architecture is "corporate branding." The originating company brand is used, and all products carry its name and all advertising speaks with the same voice. A good example of this brand architecture is the UK-based conglomerate Virgin. Virgin brands all its businesses with its name—Virgin Atlantic, Virgin Mobile, Virgin Records, and so on.

Causing Confusion Instead of Clearness

Sometimes the proliferation of brands undermines the brand architecture. Take, for example, General Motors. According to the *Harvard Business Review*:

> In the auto industry the term "Job 1" is used to denote the first car of a new model that comes off the assembly line. It's a time when all the work to create the right product and the right process either comes together or it doesn't.
>
> So it seems fitting to use the idea of Job 1 as a metaphor for what the new leadership team at GM needs to get right during the transition period. What is Job 1 at GM? They need the right brand and platform architecture to drive the company forward. Because what hobbled GM for a decade or more was

an outdated architecture that was the legacy of the founding and growth of the company.[4]

How did GM get into this mess? The *Harvard Business Review* article goes on to detail that part of the problem with GM was that it got so big that it began competing with itself instead of with "the likes of Toyota and Honda." Toyota, in particular, is used to illustrate brand architecture done properly:

> You have Toyota cars for the masses, Scion for the young-and-hip, and Lexus for luxury buyers. And that's it. Toyota vehicles are built on a relatively small number of 'platforms'— the chassis, suspension and drive train on which the shell is placed—that permit the company to offer a wide array of seemingly 'different' vehicles. And the company pays a lot of attention to sharing parts between platforms to keep production volumes up and costs down.[5]

So what does that mean for GM today? Clearly, post-recession GM will need to rethink its brand architecture, not only to operate more efficiently, but also to compete globally.

REMEMBER

- A strong foundation for your brands creates the clearness and lucidity needed for reinvention.
- Architecture is as effective in financial services, food and beverage, leisure and hospitality, or any other segment of business as it is in CPG companies—to be successful, companies and enterprises must understand how their brands fit together, what their benefits are, and how they go to market.
- Brand architecture provides a similar internal and external benefit— specifically, directness and unambiguousness of purpose for the product or service. It's not just a naming convention, but it can be the same as a company or enterprise's product architecture.

A Single Word or Symbol Can Speak Volumes

Visual impact as part of the brand experience cannot be overvalued. In a world of constant change, companies or enterprises with a strong brand as embodied and personified by their name and logo have an immediate and lasting connection with the consumer or potential customer. Reinvention begins with the distillation of the core in all elements of brand identity.

A former employee of mine (and someone I have immense respect for) recently joined a global health and wellness organization that has, among its subsidiaries, a company that provides insurance to individuals, public sector employers, and businesses of all sizes—including more than half of the Fortune 100 companies. To better align its businesses, the company was undergoing an expensive rebranding initiative. (I have agreed to keep the company name confidential, since my former employee still works there.)

At a gathering of company communications professionals this individual was attending, the marketing team had been invited in to talk about the "new brand." Before the presentation started, one of her colleagues leaned over and said to her that she couldn't believe they had to sit through a presentation on colors and font size. My ex-colleague, having been part of an integrated marketing and communications team at KPMG, knew the critical importance of a coordinated marketing and communications effort, however, and was eager to understand the key messages that would underlie this significant rebranding effort.

What she got was a presentation on fonts and colors.

Unfortunately, this ill-formed view—that marketing simply "plays" with designs and all-too-aggressively monitors font usage, size, and RGB colors while producing collateral promotional brochures and websites—is widespread and must be reinvented by any company or enterprise embarking on the important undertaking of a brand audit. As has been demonstrated time and time again, logos, brand identity elements, and overall graphic design must personify and reinforce the brand. A mistaken and singular focus on simply regulating the underpinnings of these standards can turn marketing into "brand cops" and wrongly focus them away from the brand experience.

A Rose by Any Other Name

In many ways it all starts with the name of the company or enterprise—or the name of a product or service. Dennis Hahn wrote the following for allaboutbranding.com:

> Names are the most concise distillation of an organization, product or service's essential messages, personality and brand promise. In a single word a name speaks volumes—about who and what is behind the name, and about what the audience can expect to receive in exchange for its patronage. Together with its visual manifestation, the logo, a name signals that this is an organization that merits attention, and over time it becomes a distinctive "memory tag" for storing and triggering recall of brand impressions.[1]

With a marketplace that is with every passing day more global and where a product or service can be bought or purchased via the Internet from almost any place in the world, the increasing trend over the past 30 years has been made-up names that are "new" (often the result of a combination of words or parts of words from different languages or new technologies). According to Amanda Baltazar in *Brandweek*, the more recent trend among naming experts is to follow "fashion trends":

> During the dot-com boom, there was a mania for placing an *i* or an *e*, usually in lowercase, at the beginning of a brand or product name. Before that, the previously neglected @ sign was hot (remember Gateway's 2000 "Gateway@Work" campaign or the cable Internet service Excite@Home?). And before that, tech firms in the '70s and '80s had a penchant for putting "compu-" and "-tech" at the front and back, respectively, of their brand names.[2]

Logos: The Nike Swoosh

In Veronica Napoles's book *Corporate Identity Design*, she defines the logo as a device that "helps to 'humanize' a company by presenting a face, a personality, in the form of a symbol."[3] For many who travel outside the United States, the logos of what they see as "American" brands—be it the Golden Arches, Starbucks, or Levi's—bring a sense of home, a place or experience that is comforting, reassuring, and consistent with their expectations. That is the power of a logo—to trigger memories and associations that make a brand unique to those who use it. The logo, for the consumer, is associated with something certain, something that brings security, and a sense that all is right with the world. If that's the association, the logo has done its job. Perhaps one of the best and most widely known logos in recent consumer history is the Nike swoosh. Dinesh.com details its history:

> The solid corporate logo design check was registered as a trademark in 1995. The Nike logo is an abstract wing, designed by Carolyn Davidson, [and] was an appropriate and meaningful symbol for a company that marketed running shoes. The "JUST DO IT" slogan and logo design campaign communicated such a strong point of view to their target market that the meaning for the logo design symbol evolved into a battle cry and the way of life for an entire generation. Isn't it amazing how a small symbol we call a logo design can make a company into a huge success.[4]

The name *Nike*, Greek for the winged goddess of victory, and the logo—the swoosh—both personify the brand and what it stands for to consumers. That is the power of a well-designed logo—it contributes mightily to a powerful brand identity. It becomes the symbol of the brand promise—one consumers demonstrate their belief in each time they purchase a product or service.

Graphic Design and the Brand Experience

Just for fun, right now, close your eyes and think of your favorite brands. What are your first thoughts? What are your emotions? What do you visualize? The image that immediately comes to mind is probably a logo or visual representation of that brand— the Nike swoosh or Adidas stripes, Allstate's hands, McDonald's Golden Arches, Ralph Lauren's Polo horse, the red soles of a Christian Louboutin.

This little exercise demonstrates the importance of graphic design because design defines the brand's personality and allows consumers to experience the brand in a uniform and consistent manner.

Think of the retailer Target. It has a clear visual identity instantly recognized by consumers, from its dog with the red Target eye, to its in-store promotional banners and aisle markers, to the clean typeface on its exterior store signage. Significantly (and very effectively), Target took this design to the next level when it redesigned its packaging for prescriptions. Pauline Hammerbeck analyzed the end product for *Brand Packaging*:

> Target reinvented conventional prescription bottles with a strong dose of common sense. The retailer's ClearRx packaging addressed the chief problem of traditional medicine vials: cluttered, often unintelligible labels that made medications difficult to identify and correctly use. A single, wraparound label allows for larger print on the ClearRx bottle, which features a flat front to make the important information accessible at a glance. Transparent red plastic puts the pills on view and offers an important visual refill reminder. An extra layer of safety

comes in the form of silicone rings on the neck of the bottle, which are personalized by color so individual family members can safely identify their own meds.[5]

Like Target, Apple and its use of design as a differentiator ushered in a new era in industrial design, one in which thinking about how a product will be designed is as important as any other aspect of the product development cycle.

That's the key role an innovative design can play—that of a differentiator. Crucially, one where the design reinforces the brand and its desired attributes—and buttresses, boosts, and supports the desired brand experience for the customer or prospect.

Marketing as the Brand Cop

Brand management is an essential and fundamental function of marketing, and, once a product or service has been created and designed, ensuring that the use of the logo and all other brand identity elements are properly adhered to becomes imperative. Typically, this responsibility is termed as compliance, which is perhaps best defined as follows: "the time, effort and money a company spends to ensure its employees, satellites and franchises adhere to the branding strategy and initiative throughout the entire organization."[6]

When I was at KPMG, we began a process of rebranding the firm globally in 146 countries with a brand audit that included, but was not limited to, worldwide reviews of corporate, service line, industry, recruitment, community, online, and charitable advertising; internal and external magazines; annual reports, credentials publications, and collateral brochures; white papers; surveys; case studies; "high-end" and "mid-market" proposals; team profiles and biographies; service and product briefing sheets; technical updates; large display and desktop exhibitory; invitations and "save the date" notifications; office design and environments; PowerPoint presentations; talk books; reports; letterhead, stationary, envelopes, and folders; "with compliments" cards; business cards; CDs and DVDs; e-alerts;

e-announcements; e-newsletters; e-vites; e-cards; e-promotional messages; e-surveys; websites; multimedia presentations; and, lastly, even hospitality ticket wallets and menus. At the conclusion of the audit, what we found was that, although the services offered across the globe were for the most part consistent and similar, the way KPMG presented itself to its prospects and customers, beyond its logo, was different in many countries. Sometimes even the logo had been slightly changed to match the color palette the individual member firm culturally preferred or selected to complement the local country-specific marketing efforts.

The realization that the brand was being experienced differently in these 146 countries led to the creation of the firm's first global brand identity and graphic design standards that were monitored and maintained by a team of professionals based within the marketing team's global brand management organization located in Amsterdam, London, and New York. That team trained marketing professionals in each of the firm's three regions to recognize noncompliance—in both language and design—and gave them the power to correct compliance issues or raise lingering issues to a global headquarters level. The result was that global leadership was completely invested in a "one firm" look and feel, enforcement and accountability was achieved, and the brand experience was enhanced and standardized.

REMEMBER

- Marketing owns the brand experience. As such, it must reinvent how the brand is perceived, both internally and externally, when it comes to brand personification.
- Brand personification begins with the name and continues through the logo and all other elements of brand identity. If your core essence isn't primary to the design, it must be reinvented.
- The best brand designs deliver a plethora of messages to consumers in an instant and over time. Therefore, design must not only be compelling, it must be unique and memorable.

The Whole Is Larger than Its Parts

Brand attributes define the personality of a brand—and drive purchase and desire. Knowing these characteristics is of critical importance when determining and reinventing brand positioning.

I n the end, a brand is ultimately built not only on how it is perceived by a variety of audiences but also on the many constituent parts that compose it. This includes the reputation the company, product, or service has and the attributes associated with it in the minds of customers and consumers because of direct brand experiences as well as secondary customer service interactions and third-party facilitators and channel representatives, thought leaders, media, and other key influencers—to name a few.

Some people speak about reputation management communications: these are simply brand communications, since the messages are, or should be, the same. Reputation management messaging comes from the brand positioning. The brand positioning also provides the attributes, or characteristics, of the product or service. And the sum of these attributes is what makes up the whole of a brand.

You cannot reinvent a reputation; you can rebuild it, but it takes time and effort. Blackwater knows this firsthand. The U.S. military outsourced some of its activities to Blackwater in both Afghanistan and Iraq, and the company gained a reputation in the media for being renegade mercenaries after incidents involving the deaths of civilians culminated on September 16, 2007, when Blackwater guards allegedly shot and killed 17 Iraqi civilians in Nisour Square, Baghdad.[1] Blackwater tried to turn the page by changing the company name to Xe; unfortunately, the vast majority of people still refer to the company as Blackwater and associate it with its excesses in Iraq.

Interestingly, during the BP oil spill, individual BP gas stations went so far as to petition the company to be allowed to change their name back to Amoco—a name that resonated positively with American automobile drivers. The gas stations are franchises, and the individual owners felt the anger of Americans toward the company when customers refused to purchase from them as a means of protest against the company. BP didn't agree to the name change, but this situation does show the impact of reputation and the long memory of the consumer.

Brand Attributes and Personality

If a company, product, or service were a person, how would it be described? Brand attributes are the characteristics that consumers assign to a brand or identify with it. Understanding those associations is important to reinvention. Unfortunately, for example, "renegade" and "mercenary" could be attributes assigned to Blackwater/Xe.

Attributes are especially important in high-profile, low-interest industries like financial services (with the present exception being the current interest in regulatory reform of the investment banks), where a brand's attributes are a direct outgrowth of its reputation. Often, they are a reflection of the benefits consumers or customers receive when they interact with the brand.

Take, for example, designer clothing. The attribute most typically associated with designer anything is "expensive." However, other attributes assigned to designer clothing include "well made," "high quality," and "high value." That is why people pay a great deal of money for these items of clothing. "The cost of creating those things has nothing to do with the price," said David A. Aaker, vice chairman of brand consulting firm Prophet, "It is all about who else is wearing them, who designed them and who is selling them."[2]

Brand attributes may be the same for an industry or category, but differ for products within that segment, as is shown in the subsequent example of pants (see page 83). Consider the automobile industry, which may bring to mind associations such as comfort, convenience, value, and economical transportation. However, when focusing on a particular type of car, such as an SUV, a consumer may think luxury, gas-guzzler, roomy, and expensive. If you take it one step further and think of a brand, say Volvo, the immediate characteristic that comes to mind may be safety (long promoted by the company).

Strong brands share certain attributes. A strong brand is generally perceived as:

>> Relevant: It meets people's expectations.
>> Credible: It keeps its promises.
>> Inspirational: It transcends and/or inspires the category.
>> Unique: It is set apart from other competitors in the market.

Brand Attributes' Impact on Stock Return

According to a working paper featured on the Marketing Science Institute website, a recent study demonstrated the impact of brand attributes on stock return:

Brand assets influence stock return both directly and indirectly (by impacting current earnings, which in turn affect stock returns). Among their findings:

>> A one-unit change in the Brand Asset Index is associated with a 4% change in the market value of a firm.
>> Only about ⅓ of the effect of brand assets on financial performance is reflected in current-term earnings; ⅔ reflects information about future-term performance.

>> The brand asset components reflecting relevance and vitality have direct effects on stock returns incremental to current-term earnings.

>> The brand asset components of quality, familiarity, and differentiation impact stock returns indirectly through their effects on current earnings.[3]

To return to the metaphor used previously in this book, while the brand architecture is the structure, the attributes are the furniture in the house that makes it unique. A house can be modern, French rustic, or country—whatever style reflects the character of the homeowner, or brand.

Brand Attributes: Financial Services

When I was at KPMG, we undertook a global research initiative to understand how clients perceived the firm and to create a brand positioning that more closely aligned with these perceptions. For more than three years, the U.S.-led "clarity" positioning worked exceptionally well for the firm. But in the wake of the scandals at Enron and WorldCom, it was time for reinvention. Concurrently, as a global network, KPMG was moving toward a closer affiliation and alignment with member firms overseas. Our goal became the positioning of the KPMG global brand to achieve market advantage and global consistency, leveraging the firm's strengths and creating global market differentiation.

Our quantitative research with clients and other key constituents demonstrated that the key attributes of a Big Four firm most closely associated with KPMG were "professional," "challenging," "understanding," and "successful," while the characteristics associated with these attributes included "knowledgeable," "proactive," "independent," "demanding of the highest standards," "never arrogant in approach," and "always confident in judgment." We translated these characteristics and attributes into a simple, clear global brand positioning: "Outstanding professionals working together to deliver value."

These attributes were critically important in driving satisfaction, the research demonstrated, especially with clients. In fact, the most important factor driving satisfaction was "best people with high standard," followed by "active understanding" and "value."

This new positioning was not only something that KPMG used with clients and prospects; in fact, it had as much resonance internally as it did externally. The firm's core values, upon which every KPMG professional was evaluated twice a year, were based in part on these attributes. KPMG's people were the brand's best ambassadors; they needed to understand, embody, and exhibit these attributes—and they did.

Other firms are not so fortunate. Over many years, Goldman Sachs enjoyed a pristine brand image based on its influence and power. However, in 2010, ongoing anger at Wall Street, which seemed more often than not to be aimed directly at Goldman Sachs, took a toll on its employees. In his blog for the *New York Times*, Floyd Norris relates an anecdote that perfectly sums up the new stigma, from a social gathering in which a small group of young professionals were asked what they were doing: "One young woman tried to dodge the question, talking about doing research but not mentioning an employer. After others pushed, she admitted to working for Goldman Sachs. Three years ago, such a person would have been bragging."[4]

This change in perceived brand equity shows just how deeply the ongoing Wall Street issues have penetrated the public consciousness—it's not only Main Street versus Wall Street, it's an internal battle about what Goldman Sachs is and how it is perceived by its employees. "Shame" or "embarrassment" is not what one would ever have previously associated with Goldman Sachs employees.

On the other side, an attribute definitely associated with Goldman Sachs prior to its troubles was "client-centered." That attribute was in many ways irredeemably undermined during an April 2010 Senate hearing, when Senator Susan Collins could not get a consistent answer from several Goldman leaders under oath as to whether they "had a duty to act in the best interests of their clients."[5]

And this may be costing Goldman clients. A *New York Times* article on the hearings described the seemingly contradictory structure of the company at the time of the scandal: "Goldman's many hats—trader, adviser, underwriter, matchmaker of buyers and sellers, and salesperson—has left some clients feeling bruised or so wary that they have sometimes avoided doing business with the bank."[6]

Goldman also serves as a continuing example of one important aspect of brand management: the employees of a company are often its best brand ambassadors. The *Times* article looks to an anonymous former Goldman partner to illustrate how a change in employee perspective contributed to the company's woes. According to the source:

> Under Lloyd C. Blankfein, Goldman's chief executive, and a cadre of top lieutenants who have ramped up the firm's trading operation, conflict avoidance had shifted to conflict management. . . . Along the way . . . the firm's executives have come to see customers more as competitors they trade against than as clients.[7]

Attributes are very much about these kinds of perceptions, because a brand's personality is what others think it may be. For example, a minivan will always be seen as a "Mom car," while a Mustang will always be seen as a car for those who like to go fast—a "muscle car."

REMEMBER

- Attributes are like personality characteristics; they are what a customer, prospect, or client remembers about a brand. As a result, they are an important element to reinvention.
- In determining these attributes, research what clients and targets think about the brand currently, and determine what the drivers are to their satisfaction. These should be embedded in the brand positioning and attributes.
- Attributes are a means of differentiating one brand from another. As part of the strategy, determine how the company wants the brand to be perceived, and then create attributes and a personality that meaningfully brings that perception to life.

Mind Your P's (and You Can Forget About the A's)

Marketing must drive profitable sales. It does so by understanding how to penetrate the marketplace, how to meet its target audience's preferences, and that price-value is more important than price in determining whether a reinvented product or service will be bought.

The three A's—availability, acceptability, and affordability—are taught in business school and put into action every day by marketers in companies large and small. They represent a widely accepted and embraced approach to marketing a product or service. At least they did in the old world.

In a world where marketing is focused on reinvention, three P's—penetration, preference, and price-value[1]—have replaced the three A's because they are more relevant to driving sales and to creating consumer or customer demand. That, after all, is the ultimate role of marketing—to question everything and to produce desire, induce action, and cause purchase. Without the ability to create and compel the purchase of a product or service, there is no purpose for marketing. The fashioning of artful brochures, websites, and commercials that win awards isn't sufficient to justify the investment. Marketing is a value-added, win-win game that must generate profitable sales.

Quite simply, availability does not guarantee purchase. The fact that a product sits on the shelves or a service is widely offered does not mean it will be bought. This is most evident in fashion, where each year designers in New York, Paris, London, and Milan seem removed from the reality of their customers. Remember the rapper MC Hammer? He brought us "Hammertime" and was best known for his hit "U Can't Touch This" and his ability to dance in parachute pants.

Recently designers brought back his parachute/harem pants as a fashion-forward style for women. First seen on designer runways, they were soon available in department stores. Harem pants were marketed as the chic alternative to a variety of other pants styles and were made in luxurious fabrics. However, they remained on the racks because few women could wear them well (they accentuate the hips), few viewed them as chic, and even fewer could understand why they should spend $100 on one pair of harem pants when they could get at least three or four garments for that price (and that's full price—not sales price, which most people shop today) at Old Navy. And the designers marketed these harem pants to women at the height of a recession, with no messaging about why they would be cost effective. Talk about misreading the consumer and misjudging the market opportunity.

Penetration

Penetration does not simply refer to how deeply a brand has penetrated a market. It also refers to how deeply a brand has penetrated the consciousness of the consumer. This is most visible when a brand name becomes a generic term for a product—for example, *Kleenex* for tissues, *Xerox* for copiers, or *Coke* for soft drinks.

To drive penetration, marketers need to create a desire for the product that stimulates purchase. To accomplish this, marketers must enter the consumer or customer's mind by making connections that are relevant to the environment and to their mind-set in that environment. Marketing needs to create an "ownable" environment for the product or service, which requires the right brand, right package, right configuration, right channel, and right message.

Inducing Desire

Driving this desire requires messaging via any number of platforms. Marketing must strategically choose where its advertising, promotional, and communications messages (and dollars) will run, and then make sure its choices work effectively. Twitter, which obliterates accepted filters such as time, good judgment, and common sense, is as well known for its "fail whale" (the default display when the site is down) as it is for spreading word of the heartbreaking Neda video that captured the 2009 death of a protester in Iran (more on Neda later in the book). That makes its customers hunger for an improved way to communicate—in 140 characters or less.

Social networks are not the new marketing saviors. Rather, they are simply the latest version of "over the fence" neighbors chatting. Carefully choose whether or not to participate, and do so with the expectation that the return on investment may be low. Can social networks be used to create buzz? Absolutely, but it's a double-edged sword—while social networks may create buzz, there is no proof they can create sales or even a brand.

However, there is anecdotal evidence that Twitter, essentially a microblogging site, can negatively impact a movie—as Sacha Baron Cohen learned with his movie *Bruno*. According to a Reuter's story from July 17, 2009:

> Last Friday, actor Sacha Baron Cohen's gay-themed comedy *Bruno*, which was distributed by Universal Pictures, made an impressive one-day debut of $14.4 million at U.S. and Canadian box offices, but the next day it suffered a large single-day drop, falling 39 percent to $8.8 million. Media reports speculated that *Bruno* suffered from the "Twitter effect," meaning audiences reacted quickly online to raunchy scenes of sex and nudity, scaring people away.[2]

Notably, marketers may be reinventing the cell phone as a research tool. Recently, various companies have introduced the idea of using iPhone applications (or "apps") like Foursquare, a location-based service that offers rewards to its participants as they reach various locations, to drive sales. B. Bonin Bough, director of social and emerging media for PepsiCo, described in the *New York Times* how the application was being used:

> If you check into work, then you leave work, you check into a bank and then you check into a store, that's a behavior that, in aggregate, we might use to transform the way we market to you in the offline world. . . . We might see dayparts that are more likely for you to check out of some place and go to the store, and we might do advertising during that specific daypart in that specific place. . . . We believe it's a real, new opportunity to transform loyalty programs in a way that we haven't done before.[3]

Will this drive desire to purchase or despair at the intrusive nature of the app? While many believe technology has made people's lives easier (What could be better than getting a savings coupon just in time?), it also has made lives busier and more demanding, and at the same time more complicated, interconnected, and, increasingly, frantic. Almost everyone now has numerous online "touch points" for different types of Internet-centered activities. They have company e-mail for business contacts; use Amazon for online expenditures; do social networking on Facebook; update friends on Twitter; and have Nike+ track daily runs, including duration, pace, and calories, among many other things.

Given these new interdependencies and the evolving nature of personally applied technology, it is important that marketers recognize that when it comes to technology, early adopters are not only the tech savvy—they are everyone. You are they. The Imagining the Internet Center at Elon University and the Pew Research Center's Internet & American Life Project found that 76 percent of experts agreed with the statement: "By 2020, people's use of the Internet has enhanced human intelligence; as people are allowed unprecedented access to more information they become smarter and make better choices."[4] In view of this far-reaching conclusion, using technology smartly in marketing makes it significantly more effective, more efficient, and more immediate—today and critically into the future.

The Penetration Master

Apple is a master at penetration—from iPods to iPhones to iPads to its reinvented Macintosh line now better known as MacBooks. Nowhere is this better substantiated and confirmed then in the *New York Times* story "Apple Passes Microsoft as No. 1 in Tech."[5] The story affirms Apple's ascendancy and attempts to pinpoint how it happened:

> This changing of the guard caps one of the most stunning turnarounds in business history for Apple, which had been given up for dead only a decade earlier, and its co-founder and visionary chief executive, Steven P. Jobs. The rapidly rising value attached to Apple by investors also heralds an important cultural shift: Consumer tastes have overtaken the needs of business as the leading force shaping technology.[6]

Apple creates a pervasive environment that compels and drives the consumer to buy and matches it with unparalleled manufacturing and distribution prowess and exquisite industrial product design. More often than not, the company starts with well-placed leaks to select reporters about "something new" that Apple is working on. That usually happens three or four months before the annual MacWorld convention. By the time MacWorld rolls around in February each year, speculation is running wild in the press and on technology blogs about Apple's latest product innovation. And with Apple, it's always about reinvention-led innovation—that's its core essence, and the key attribute consumers associate with the brand.

Apple's introduction of the newest creation is normally conducted at MacWorld by Steve Jobs, the founder and CEO of the company, who is viewed by many as the genius nerd who is also cool—a dichotomy in itself. (In early 2011, concurrent with the release of first quarter financial performance of record sales and profits resulting from all product lines, Apple also announced that Steve Jobs, Apple's visionary and iconic leader, was taking another extended leave of absence from the company to focus on recurring health issues related to a rare form of pancreatic cancer.) Most recently, Apple's iPad launch was live-blogged by numerous publications, including the *New York Times*, and was a trending topic on Twitter.

Then Apple builds anticipation through its advertising, which makes it seem that if you, the consumer, don't have the latest Apple invention, you are missing out on a secret that everyone else knows. Finally, with the introduction, there is a rush to buy— at Apple stores. It is there where Apple has reached the marketing apex. The store is a cool reflection of the company. It's all white— like many of the products. Consumers can touch, explore, and otherwise interact with the products, and the people who help the prospective buyer are knowledgeable but never pushy.

Most recently, the iPad introduction in April 2010 proved the truth and effectiveness of this approach to reinvention. More than 300,000 iPads were sold on day one. The product sold out in preorders, and it was basically unavailable in Apple stores—at a price point of approximately $500 each—an amazing launch for any consumer product. In fact, on account of the high prelaunch demand, Apple had to take a step unheard of in its own recent history, detailed in a company statement: "Faced with this surprisingly strong U.S. demand, we have made the difficult decision to postpone the international launch of iPad by one month, until the end of May."[7]

As it relates to other Apple products, Apple's brilliance and effectiveness at penetration is easily seen—iPods and their white earbuds are ubiquitous on the streets and subways of any major metropolitan area, as well as in airports, cars, and on jogging paths—anywhere that people listen to music. And if you don't have an iPod you may have one of its offspring—the Nano, the Shuffle, or the iPod Touch, for example. The iPhone would have been without a doubt even more ever-present if it were originally available on networks other than AT&T's—and now that the iPhone for Verizon has become a reality, it will continue to grow the brand dramatically. Verizon's iPhone comes on top of their late 2010 announcement offering iPad service—and the data plans will be cheaper than those currently offered by AT&T.

On June 7, 2010, the iPhone 4 was unveiled and represents the biggest reinvention of the iPhone since the original 2007 release. The iPhone 4 is certainly a radical departure from prior versions. With its flat glass back and stainless steel edges, it looks more like a Braun appliance than a cell phone. Breakthrough advancements among numerous new capabilities include live video chat via FaceTime, a new app developed by Apple that makes video teleconferencing a consumer reality.

However, Apple does have a new competitor on its horizon: Google, which itself is excellent at achieving penetration. In a *New York Times* profile of the emerging Google/Apple rivalry, the paper reports that Google is "battling Apple in mobile devices with its Android operating system, and mobile advertising." The *Times* goes beyond the mobile device market and profiles each company's position on a number of technological fronts:

> Google, with a market cap of $151.43 billion, also appeared to leap ahead of Apple in a new potentially important area, Internet-connected televisions. And Google is steering consumers toward yet a new model of computing in which Internet applications, rather than iPhone or desktop applications, rule.[8]

Ma Bell—the Only Game in Town

Once upon a time, AT&T didn't have to worry about penetration, preference, or price-value—it was the only game in town. It was Ma Bell, and every American used it in their home and at the office, and only in those locations—not while walking the street, riding a bus, driving a car, or running between appointments. Then the telecommunications industry segment was transformed almost overnight by the divestiture of the Bell companies in the late 1980s as required by an antitrust ruling of the Supreme Court.

This breakup led to a surge in competition in the telecommunications industry. The "Baby Bells," new regional operating companies formerly part of AT&T, were now all competing with each other as well as with other new competition. Concurrently, technology advancements enabled the creation (and ultimate proliferation) of cell phones. First, there was the "brick" phone, then a series of phones developed by Motorola that culminated with the "Flip" and "Moto" handheld devices, then the globalization of wireless cell technology led by Nokia and a proliferation of other competitors and technology platforms.

And AT&T was left behind. In fact, it was sold to SBC Corporation, and its wireless business was sold to Cingular. However, the AT&T name was kept—AT&T Inc. for the overall business and AT&T Wireless for the cell phone business—because of the inherent but latent value of the deeply embedded AT&T brand in the consumer's consciousness. But it was still viewed as a slow network, with questionable coverage for a high price.

And then came the iPhone.

Recognizing that it had missed the boat in the wireless wars, AT&T Wireless partnered with Apple to create the newest, trendiest cell phone on the market. With that exclusive partnership, AT&T quickly transformed its reputation to one of being "cool." Most important, this partnership drove sales: AT&T Wireless gained a plethora of new subscribers when the iPhone was introduced in 2007.

The cost to jump in the ring with Apple was considerable. According to the *New York Times*, AT&T paid Apple an "unusually high subsidy on top of the $199 and $299 paid by iPhone buyers."[9]

The investment paid off. The *Times* reports that in the first quarter of 2010, less than three years after it launched the iPhone, AT&T's profit margin was up considerably (26 percent over the previous year), as were overall accounts:

> The company activated 1.6 million iPhones on its network in the quarter. And more than 640,000 of those customers were new to AT&T's network. That represents three-quarters of the net addition of 875,000 new postpaid consumer accounts in the quarter. (AT&T added 325,000 more net business and prepaid wireless accounts in the quarter, as well.)[10]

The *Times* goes on to monetize the extended value of each new activation (thanks to high data costs), but also makes it clear that the depth of AT&T's penetration is directly linked to the exclusivity of its agreement with Apple: 2.5 million new customers a year representing $700 million in operating profits are what's at stake, and as that exclusive window draws to an end with the announcement that Verizon will start selling iPhones in early 2011,[11] AT&T now has its work cut out for it and may need to reinvent its strategy once again. And, the strategic review may be under way. AT&T announced in late December 2010 that it was buying QualComm in an effort to strengthen its 4G network.[12] iPhone users have consistently complained about the perceived weakness of the AT&T network for placing calls and for getting Web access. While the purchase of QualComm is a step in the right direction, it remains to be seen if this is the beginning of a reinvention or a panicked reaction to Verizon's new relationship with Apple.

Preference Is as Emotional as It Is Rational

Going forward, the most interesting marketing battle in the handheld telecommunications segment may be between the iPad and Amazon's Kindle. For a while, Amazon, which does little or no advertising, had the e-book reader market to itself. Akin to the Palm Pilot in its infancy, Kindle is a purveyor of words in black and white.

The Kindle is not cool and fun; it is austere, practical, and workmanlike. But it is convenient and reliable. By comparison, the iPad is fun, and using it feels somehow rewarding; most important for readers, it harkens back to the experience of reading an actual printed book. It is that difference that has kept Kindle from the penetration level the iPad will probably reach. It's about the experience—the pervasive experience—of reading.

However, the Kindle has one advantage over the iPad: because of its lack of bells and whistles, it is easily read in the sunlight, unlike the iPad, which is difficult if not impossible to read outdoors in the sun. This has given an opening to the Kindle, which Amazon immediately capitalized on in its advertising. (For the record, Amazon, which as noted earlier does not do a great deal of advertising, began fairly aggressive television outreach for the Kindle in the months before and after the iPad was introduced and released.)

Apple's introduction of the iPad was, as always, innovative, and while there were complaints—it had no USB ports, for example—its large color screen, the way it "turns" book pages, and its multiple functions (e-mail, Word, and so on) place it far ahead of the Kindle.

Additionally, the applications or "apps" that Apple has made its exclusive purview for the iPhone and iPod Touch can be used on the iPad, and video can also be viewed. In short, the iPad is a handheld entertainment center—something the current Kindle cannot compete against, nor can any of the other e-book readers on the market (or, for that matter, the entire category of subcompact computers called netbooks).

Amazon's Kindle also points to another shortcoming of the three A's: acceptability is not a differentiator. The Kindle is an acceptable e-book reader. However, preference is the indisputable differentiator. While the Kindle is acceptable, the iPad is preferable (albeit at a higher price) because of the experience it provides the consumer.

If "acceptable" isn't enough, then it seems the battle has been joined. Amazon responded to the iPad with a new, lighter model, referred to in the media as the "Kindle 3." With an updated and improved design that eliminated much of the beige plastic that bordered its predecessor while maintaining the same screen dimensions, a lighter weight more conducive to reading, and a reduced price point, David Pogue of the *New York Times* praised the new Kindles as "everything the iPad will never be: small, light and inexpensive."[13]

The Apple-Amazon e-reader war is, in effect, two core essences at odds. Apple is all about cool fun: giving you more than you need, but making you want it. Amazon is about helping you locate what you need—and little else. Amazon shoppers can find anything they want on the site, from food to clothing to shoes to books. It is about the necessities of life, not about browsing. Apple gives you ease of access to what it considers the necessities—and somehow manages to always make you come back for more. You want to browse the app store, or iTunes, to see what's new and what you may want but probably don't absolutely need. Apple has an aura—it constantly reinvents itself. Amazon, once revolutionary, doesn't—it remains tethered to its core. And its core is convenience and utility.

The Value of a Value Proposition

The key to creating preference is knowing the value proposition of a product or service. If marketing doesn't know the value proposition, it can't determine new ways to leverage the product or service, or to expand its differentiation.

Sadly, most companies don't know their value proposition, and they don't know what actually motivates purchase intent for their products or services. So, without knowing how to exploit current opportunities or to build on them, companies exchange strategy for "new ideas." Unfortunately, a value proposition is not something discussed (more often than not) in corporate hallways. A value proposition is an examination and quantified assessment of the benefits, costs, and worth that an organization can deliver to customers and other constituent segments within and outside of the organization. A value proposition does not show up in marketing materials; rather, it serves to guide marketing and marketing communications and underlies all the messaging that is created. The messages must always communicate a benefit to the target audience; these benefits result from the articulation of the value proposition.

If Consumers Find Value, They Will Pay the Price

In building or reinventing a brand, while differentiation may be a motivating factor, preference is crucial. Consumers will pay a higher price for the brands they prefer. Simply, affordability is not about price; it's about the value derived from the product or service by the consumer or customer.

This is particularly applicable to Apple, which uses an interesting method to drive value. Michael Gartenberg at Macworld .com discusses Apple's approach:

> The key to Apple's success is that the company often takes the time to explain things to the consumer that no other vendor bothers to do. By keeping a laser focus on key features and introducing them one at a time over a period of years, Apple

taught and evangelized everything the consumer needed to know to understand the iPad from day one. Without that foundation, it's not likely the product would have been nearly the success it has been.[14]

Then comes the truest line in this look at Apple:

The greatest products in the world don't get anywhere without telling a good story. The ability for Apple to tell that story and then allow consumers to get hands-on experience with products has become a powerful combination that's allowed Apple to succeed where others have failed miserably.[15]

The Apple-Microsoft rivalry is a perfect example of this failure. Microsoft is, without a doubt, the behemoth. But consumers don't brag about upgrading to Office 2007 like they do about getting the newest iPhone on a 4G network. With Apple, it's about a total experience, not a product. With Microsoft it's about—well, it's about attempting to reinvent itself. If any company has lost its way, Microsoft has. Its advertising featuring a broad spectrum of typical users promoting that "Windows 7 was my idea" pales when compared to Apple's creativity and pervasiveness. The idea that Microsoft listens to its customers is greeted with skepticism, while Apple's intrusiveness is welcomed—as a window into a new world.

Brand Versus Commodity

Emphasizing value builds a brand; emphasizing price builds a commodity. This is perhaps best seen in everyday staples for the home, such as paper towels or toilet paper. Consumers often buy these products at the sale price, not seeing much of a differentiation or distinction between brands. Indeed, they may go for the store or private label brand if it comes to saving money.

This has also been seen in the "Great Pizza Wars of 2010," when Pizza Hut made all of its pizzas—any size, any toppings—available for $10 each. That was an amazing, if not controversial, pricing strategy initially developed by franchisees, since large pies at other fast-food outlets may cost up to $18 or more. But success does come with a price. Pizza Hut has been so successful in using this discounted price promotional strategy that the company has been unable, as of this writing, to replicate its success with in-market tests of other incentives. Unfortunately, it didn't (and still doesn't as of this date) have a longer-term alternative to move the customer to a non-price-driven platform.

Notwithstanding this fact, in April 2010, *Restaurant News* reported the findings of a survey on pizza by Technomic, a Chicago-based food-industry consulting firm:

> Nearly one-fifth of those surveyed said price, coupons or discount promotions influenced their pizza buying decisions. . . . 62 percent of consumers polled said cravings drove their most recent purchase of away-from-home pizza, compared with 25 percent of respondents who went out for pizza because it's more convenient than cooking at home.[16]

Technomic executive vice president Darren Tristano noted that in an average month more than 90 percent of U.S. consumers eat pizza, and for companies to capture more of the market, "chains must appeal to consumers' sense of taste with bold flavors and diverse offerings." Tristano further details his proposed strategy:

> Operators and suppliers will want to consider what they can do to elicit consumer cravings through adding new items to their menus and emphasizing them through their marketing message. . . . Differentiation through pizzas that feature unique flavors and taste combinations that consumers cannot purchase elsewhere or make at home will likely help support this effort. Positioning pizza as a meal solution that is easy, convenient and affordable will resonate with many consumers.[17]

Once a product becomes a commodity, it becomes all about price point, not essence. Differentiation is lost, and your competition wins because it's a level playing field. Products and services must be reinvented before they become commodities to ensure brand loyalists stay that way—and aren't distracted by a price war.

Value and the Recession

The audience that is most often considered to be the most value-oriented, especially during a time of recession, is mothers. Female-led households were especially hard-hit by the recession, as these statistics show:

>> In 2008, seven out of ten mothers with children under 18 years old were in the labor force. More than half of all mothers usually worked full time last year.

>> As of April 2009, nearly one million working-age female heads of household wanted a job but could not find one.

>> One out of every ten women maintaining a family is unemployed, which exceeds the highest rate (9.0 percent) experienced during the 2001 recession and the "jobless recovery" that followed. The ranks of female heads of household who are unemployed or "marginally attached" to the labor force has grown across all demographic groups, with women of color faring the worst. Black and Hispanic women in this group are currently experiencing unemployment at rates of 13.3 percent and 11.0 percent, respectively.[18]

As a result, female heads of household don't necessarily look at price as much as value, and they know that better-made clothing, though a little more expensive, may last longer than the cheaper versions of the same things. Similarly, they may not see the value in buying a specialized brand of spaghetti, for example, when they can get something similar on sale.

For these reasons, as well as for many others, price should be communicated in context of other brand values—never in isolation. Consumers need reasons—functional and nonfunctional, rational and emotional—to buy a brand. These reasons must come from the brand positioning. And the brand positioning should just be one component of an overall brand architecture.

How a brand is positioned is crucial to driving preference. Take, for example, Harvard University. It positions itself as accepting only the crème de la crème of graduates. Its value and cachet is derived from its history, and from the many well-known graduates of its ivy-covered halls and their high-paying, powerful positions. If a graduating high school senior has the ability to make it into Harvard, price often makes no difference. The value of a Harvard education far outweighs the price paid to get it.

Perhaps one of the best and most recent high-profile examples of price value is NBC. Once the home of "Must See TV," NBC Universal was bought by Comcast not for its network's stature, but for its cable channels. As a *New York Times* article said, "At every turn, Comcast has emphasized to its own shareholders that the deal's purpose is to gain control over NBC Universal's fast-growing cable channels. The writer and humorist John Dillon observed . . . that in the 2,742-word news release about the deal, the broadcast network was not mentioned until word 2,170. There is even talk of changing NBC Universal's name to play down the broadcast association."[19]

What this demonstrates is that there is an astonishingly diminished value of the NBC network as compared to the cable channels in the overall brand portfolio. The emotional brand connection NBC had with its viewers was diminished or destroyed not only by competitors, including cable channels, but also by the network's own short-term decisions—to program four nights of "Deal or No Deal" and five nights of Jay Leno at 10:00 P.M. (Eastern and Pacific times). The impetus for this type of programming from a corporate perspective was saving money in a changing competitive marketplace. However, it never seemed to dawn on the honchos at NBC that they could still create preference and then drive value by producing programs that consumers loyally watch, and then charging higher advertising prices for them, as it had in its heyday. The network went to the lowest common denominator, and it lost its well of goodwill and its pervasive connection with the television viewer.

Doing so may also have cost Jeff Zucker, the head of NBC Universal, his job. When Zucker resigned in September 2010, it was no surprise. It was seen by many as an inevitable component of Comcast's deal that was no doubt fueled by the perceived loss of network value under his watch. Comcast now faces an interesting challenge at NBC, which itself is in need of reinvention.

The Old Reliables

Marketers often speak about taking a holistic approach to the marketplace, but fall back on the old reliables—specifically the three A's—when the time comes. However, marketers should be held to the holistic approach, since it is as experiential as it is value driven.

Penetration, preference, and price-value should be the key drivers of any marketing plan. Much thought should be given to the brand's positioning, how it relates to other brands under the corporate umbrella and to other competitive brands in the marketplace, and what is at the brand's core. That core is what keeps consumers and customers coming back to buy—it drives preference and price-value. As long as marketers never lose sight of the core, the brand can continue to grow through reinvention while holding onto its base.

REMEMBER

- Penetration creates the pervasiveness for the product or service that stimulates purchase.
- Acceptability is not a differentiator. If you don't know your company's or your brand's value proposition, you can't determine new ways to leverage it or expand on it to create differentiation and drive preference.
- Emphasizing value creates a brand; emphasizing price creates a commodity.

Do as I Do, Not as I Say

**Recognize that consumers and even customers
sometimes say one thing and do another; as a result, it
is imperative that marketers use both stated and derived
research findings to determine reinvention plans.**

Actions speak louder than words. That's not just a cliché;
it's true, nowhere more so than in marketing. And time and
time again companies discover that what the consumer
says is not necessarily what the consumer, in fact, does.

Perception Is Reality

There can be no doubt that in today's world most consumers—and certainly most parents—put their greatest value and
importance on their time spent with their families, since, in
study after study, family time is invariably perceived as the commodity in shortest supply. But is it really? A *New York Times* blog
reported the findings of a study conducted by two economists at
the University of California, San Diego, in which a dozen surveys
conducted between 1965 and 2007 on "how Americans say they
use their time" were analyzed. The study found that "mothers
and fathers alike are doing a better job than they think, spending
far more time with their families than did parents of earlier gen-
erations." The *Times* went on to report the following:

The amount of child care time spent by parents at all income
levels—and especially those with a college education—has

risen "dramatically" since the mid-1990s. . . . Before 1995, mothers spent an average of about 12 hours a week attending to the needs of their children. By 2007, that number had risen to 21.2 hours a week for college-educated women and 15.9 hours for those with less education.[1]

That said, working parents still perpetually agonize that they don't see enough of their children because of other demands on their time—despite the evidence to the contrary. One reason for the discrepancy may be technology's role in the lives of modern parents. While technology benefits consumers by giving them more time with family and friends away from the office, in reality it is more of a tether. They are not getting time back—they are having time taken away because they are constantly checking their BlackBerry or iPhone and responding to texts or e-mails at dinner, soccer practice, or at home late into the night.

"Stated" Research

Let's take the recent Domino's versus Papa John's pizza challenge as another example of the difference between perception and reality. Domino's, unfortunately known as making a bland pizza, changed the recipe its pizza makers used to include more cheese, fresh tomatoes, and otherwise increase the taste potential and satisfaction of its hungry buyers. It then directly challenged Papa John's in advertisements by going back to consumers who had chosen their competitor's pie, asking them to taste the new Domino's Pizza, and having them state, for the camera, how much better Domino's now tasted.

What the commercials did not ask was if that taste would not only influence but change their purchasing habits, or if they would continue to call for the pizza they were comfortable with and had been ordering for a while. Importantly, what a consumer tells a researcher is not necessarily an accurate reflection of his or her actual real-world actions. That's why marketers should always look to and follow the actions of consumers or customers, and not simply take them at their word. Despite its low price, it is my unsubstantiated belief that consumers still associate Domino's with bland pizza, and their buying patterns haven't changed. Unfortunately, many marketers still rely on focus groups and their qualitative "stated" findings for definitive research, and they tend to take what people say as fact.

This frequently happens, for example, with elections in the United States. Michael Bloomberg's election to a third term as mayor of New York City is a perfect example. Mayor Bloomberg invested more than $85 million of his own money into his campaign, and he was on pace to spend well more than $100 million, outspending his opponent, Comptroller William Thompson Jr., by a 14-to-1 margin.[2] Many in the New York press had given the election little or no coverage, assuming that Mayor Bloomberg would once again trounce his opponent. But that's not what happened. The press and pollsters underestimated voters' annoyance if not outright anger with the mayor's circumventing the two-term limit that New York City had previously put in place, and they seemed to resent the amount of money he spent to ensure a victory and his reelection. Mr. Bloomberg won, but by a 51 to 46 percent margin. As the *New York Times* put it, "Still, the margin seemed to startle Mr. Bloomberg's aides and the city's political establishment, which had predicted a blowout. Published polls in the days leading up to the election suggested that the mayor would win by as many as 18 percentage points; four years ago, he cruised to reelection with a 20 percent margin."[3]

Stated Versus Derived

Marketers must take the next step to determine actual customer or consumer preference. In "stated versus derived" research, a marketer must look at preference, habits, and value. By mapping the data for stated versus derived results, a marketer can determine which benefits and attributes are both important and motivating—and those that most correlate to actual action.

Before I joined a marketing strategy consultancy as president, the company worked with a well-known ski resort to determine how to get more visitors to its location. What the team learned was that functional benefits like price and access to great ski runs were important, but they were not the actual purchase drivers. In fact, the real influencers of purchase were the emotional benefits—the experience of the ski resort overall. Skiers didn't need to be sold on skiing; instead, the consultants recommended that the overall target audience needed to be sold on both "on and off" mountain activities, and the resort needed to target younger, more active skiers intrigued by this area's mountains. They redefined and reinvented the experience of skiing for this resort.

With this reinvention came recognition. The most respected industry trade magazine rated this client as the number one ski resort in America, up from number four and higher than any other ranking the client had ever received. By the end of the inaugural season, which unfortunately turned out to be a terrible year for snow in the West, skiers' visits were down only 4 percent, while all other ski resorts were down 15 to 20 percent.

Very simply, derived benefits are based on consumer or customer *actions*—something that marketers are paid to deliver in the form of growth and profitable revenue; stated benefits are merely the first step in determining these purchase drivers. As a marketer, you must know your customers and understand what motivates them to act; only then can you differentiate your brand.

The Credibility Gap

One needs to go no further than the New Coke anecdote introduced in Principle #2 to understand that millions of dollars can be misspent by a company when consumers say one thing but do something else entirely—where their actions are not in keeping with their words.

Some further background for this well-intended but colossal misjudgment adds a significant component to the story. Prior to the launch of New Coke, Coca-Cola conducted several taste tests with focus groups. In fact, according to an article by John Greenwald in *Time* magazine:

Coke embarked on the most exhaustive and far-reaching research program in its history. In all, nearly 200,000 consumers were asked to participate over a three-year period. The results were close, but they persuaded Coke executives that they were on the right track. When asked to compare unmarked beverages, 55 percent of the drinkers favored New Coke over old Coke. When both drinks were identified, the margin rose 6 points. . . . As Coke now concedes, its test marketing was flawed. Among other things, Coca-Cola neglected to inform consumers that choosing New Coke meant saying farewell to old Coke.[4]

Interestingly, today the Coca-Cola website has a slightly different, some might say revisionist, perspective on this debacle: "The events of 1985 changed forever the dynamics of the soft-drink industry and the success of The Coca-Cola Company, as the Coca-Cola brand soared to new heights and consumers continued to remember the love they have for Coca-Cola."[5]

REMEMBER

- People may say what they mean; however, they sometimes don't mean and act upon what they say.
- Marketers must dig deeper to better understand consumer and customer preferences that will help drive reinvention.
- "Stated" preferences are not necessarily the benefits consumers will pay to own; they may be aspirational.
- "Derived" measures tell marketers not only what consumers or customers prefer, they also can predict actions—what consumers and customers will pay to own.
- Derived measures are an important aspect of reinvention; they can help marketers understand how to position their product or service so that it optimally connects with the target audience.

RULE THREE

THERE ARE MANY CHOICES BUT ONLY ONE CUSTOMER

N THE new age of marketing, marketers must understand now more than ever how their messages, executions, offers, and incentives are best and most effectively received (via advertising, print, direct mail, e-mail, social networks, or other means) and ultimately responded to and acted upon by the consumer or prospect—and reinforced by the customer service brand experience.

Notably, in today's data-driven, technology-oriented world there is simply no excuse for not monitoring and rigorously evaluating return on investment (ROI), nor is there one for treating the customer as anything but an individual who may become a brand loyalist. ROI is dependent on having a clear strategy built on a brand's essence, positioning, and a comprehensive understanding of the customer as a person and not a number.

Reinvention begins with reinventing the relationship with the customer that results in an all-encompassing brand experience that drives customer loyalty and, more important, repeat sales for a very long time. That is why both an understanding of the relevance of a brand's positioning and an understanding of the brand perceptions that create repeatable events and repeat purchases are so important in this new landscape.

Strategy Is the Heart, but Measurement Is the Lifeblood

Marketing is a data-driven science; to reinvent a company or enterprise, or a brand, product, or service successfully you must have a strategic plan with unyielding metrics that justify return on investment for every dollar spent on programs.

Strategy should inform everything a marketer does.

Strategy begins at the top. There should be an overall strategy for the company or enterprise that says who or what the company or enterprise is and what it wants to be. That strategy should set a clear vision, and any marketing plan should provide a means of successfully and profitably making that vision a reality.

Each product or service will have its own individual product or service line strategy. However, these strategies should fit seamlessly within the singular corporate strategy and vision as well as within the overarching marketing strategy, and they should clearly state what role this particular product or service plays in reaching the goals set by the company or enterprise. As the first step in disseminating the brand, this form of clarity is imperative. The strategy also must help create presence in the marketplace, relevance with users, differentiation from competition, credibility, product usage, and associative imagery. Very simply, it must be holistic—and it must above all else be measurable.

Marketing as an Investment

Marketing is crucial to the success of a business. For this reason, the result must be measurable. If a plan does not contain metrics, it fails before it even begins.

Just like any other business function, marketing should be viewed as an investment, not as an expense. Expenses are constantly managed, and cuts are often mandated from the top. A company or enterprise is investing in the belief that marketing can help achieve its vision; marketers must prove, through plans and associated metrics, that marketing can—and will—do so.

Companies make money only when they complete a successful and profitable transaction with a buyer—whether the buyer is a wholesaler, retailer, customer, or end consumer—not when they simply complete the manufacturing process. And the one department other than sales that helps a company or enterprise sell a product or service is marketing. Slashing marketing and diverting the dollars elsewhere may solve some problems in the short term, but in the long term it creates more problems. Many more.

Marketing is an investment, albeit a short-, medium-, and long-term one.

During the Great Recession as well as earlier economic downturns, we read time and again of how companies decimated their marketing departments, often cutting them completely. At the same time, press reports and analyst accounts continued to say that sales lagged.

A recent exception is Wal-Mart. Though the company was impacted by the recession, it did better than most other retailers. The reason for that is fairly simple—Wal-Mart as a company knows who it is . . . well, at least it does now.

In 2005 to 2006, under a new chief marketing officer, Wal-Mart had a very brief flirtation with designer branding and positioning as a higher-end retailer, directly competing with Target. It advertised in *Vogue* and other fashion magazines and offered trendy clothing aimed at a younger demographic.

And it tanked completely.

For a variety of reasons, Wal-Mart corrected its course; one of the changes it made was to name Stephen F. Quinn as its new chief marketing officer. Quinn, a marketer from PepsiCo's $10 billion Frito-Lay division, and new merchant leaders understood the essence of the retail concept Sam Walton had created: Wal-Mart is a discount store that saves people money to help them live their lives better. It does not compete with Target or other retailers because it is one of a kind.

Wal-Mart went back to its future just as the recession hit. The company reinvented itself. In its legacy role, it was ideally positioned when Americans began looking for ways to save money yet still get a good value. (Value, while almost always important, is of enormous consequence during recessionary times, never more so than when people are losing homes and jobs concurrently.)

Wal-Mart was smart enough to course correct before real long-term damage was done to its brand or to its relationship with its target audience. Its strategy remains unchanged, but it has continued to reinvent itself and expanded organically to include grocery items in its stores. As the top seller of groceries in the United States, its marketing stresses the fact that by shopping for food at its stores—something Wal-Mart is not historically known for—consumers can provide a good, healthy meal for their families at a big savings. Wal-Mart made consumers aware that they can get both USDA Grade A steaks and the well-known brands families use every day for less. And it reiterated and reinforced the brand promise that by shopping at Wal-Mart, an individual can "spend less and live better."

Wal-Mart learned the hard way that a company cannot stray too far from its core and remain consistently successful. With a minor blip, it has always pursued a strategy that celebrated its essence.

On the other hand, there is Sears. Sears is, very simply, a company that grew with the United States. Sears Roebuck is an American brand created as a mail-order company in 1886 by Richard Sears. In 1887, Alvah C. Roebuck joined him, and in 1893 the corporate name of the firm became Sears, Roebuck and Co.

At the time Sears was started, farmers in rural America were selling their crops for cash and buying what they needed from rural general stores. Thanks to volume buying, made possible by the railroads and post office, and later to rural free delivery and parcel post, Sears Roebuck with its variety of products offered an alternative to high-priced rural stores. As a result, in the 1890s Sears prospered: sales in 1893 topped $400,000; two years later, they exceeded $750,000.

Sears continued as solely a mail-order business until 1925. Then, as cars and modern roads become more available, Sears's rural customers were no longer limited to shopping by catalog. More important, the era of the American city was beginning: the cities were growing up, and Sears's rural customers were abandoning the farm for the factory. In 1900 the rural population still outnumbered the urban population, but by 1920 the situation was reversed.

Sears grew from a mail-order business to 192 stores in 1928, to 319 stores in 1929, and to 400 stores in 1933. During one 12-month period in the late 1920s, stores opened on the average of one every other business day. When two huge stores opened in one city on the same day, more than 120,000 people visited them during the first 12 hours they were open. With this growth, Sears began developing its own brands, including its renowned Craftsman, Kenmore, and DieHard product lines.

In 1931 Sears's retail sales topped mail-order sales for the first time. Stores accounted for 53.4 percent of total sales of more than $180 million. Despite the Great Depression, Sears continued to open stores during the 1930s. When war broke out in 1941, more than 600 stores were operating. World War II called a halt to Sears's retail expansion.

Brand expansion, however, was another option altogether. And it was an option that Sears ultimately pursued with an uneven range of success.

Allstate Insurance Co. was launched as a wholly owned Sears subsidiary in 1931. Its name was taken from a Sears line of automobile tires. At first, Allstate operated only by mail. However, by 1933 management discovered that most sales were being made in smaller towns where the catalog business was booming, while the large metropolitan markets were not responding. As a result, Allstate pioneered a bold idea—the installation of sales locations in Sears stores. Thus began Sears's flirtation with the financial services industry—one that muddied its brand and ultimately took the company away from its core.

In 1981, Sears acquired the Dean Witter Reynolds Organization, Inc., and Coldwell Banker & Company to create the Sears Financial Network (where I learned firsthand as a young consultant advising Coldwell Banker the important lesson that "more is not necessarily better for the customer"). The following year, Sears formed a world trading company. The corporation—plus the Discover Card introduced in 1985—grew into the 1990s, with revenues reaching $59 billion in 1992. That year Sears announced it would again reshape the company to give it greater strength and marketing focus and to give its shareholders a better return on investment.

As part of this restructuring, the Sears Merchandise Group, reorganized around its apparel, home, and automotive businesses, closed many of its underperforming retail locations, including some mall-based stores.

In early 1993, Sears sold Coldwell Banker Residential Services, the Sears Mortgage Banking Group, and the Homart Development Company. Total proceeds from these transactions, about $4 billion, were used to reduce overall corporate debt. With its diversified companies divested, Sears, Roebuck and Co. returned to its retailing roots.[1] Unfortunately, that return was unsuccessful. Sears had lost its way and, more important, lost its connection to its retailing customers, who didn't recognize (or prefer) the Sears brand any longer.

In 2005 Sears merged with Kmart into Sears Holdings, and, unfortunately, it has failed to recapture much of its faded glory.

The lesson of Sears as compared to Wal-Mart is simple. A company's business strategy must celebrate the brand's essence by clearly defining the following:

>> Target: Who do you want to use your brand?
>> Competitive framework: Where do you want your brand to compete?
>> Key benefit: What does your brand stand for?
>> Support: Why should users believe your key benefit?

Creating a Marketing Strategy

When reinventing a brand, marketers must build their marketing strategies on brand positioning—an understanding of what a brand is at its core and how that core impacts key audiences. This form of positioning recognizes that brands are organic—they change, and new facets are continually being discovered and refined.

To be successful, marketing must constantly test the brand's positioning to ensure that it resonates with the target audience. Consumers won't pay for what they don't value, and critical to value is an understanding that it drives desire to purchase. Reinvention that emphasizes value creates disproportionate brand loyalty.

The critical starting point remains strategy for both business and marketers. Today, in many companies and enterprises, the marketing department is given a budget, and then those dollars more often than not are deployed against various programs linked to certain products or services. Conversely, reinvention mandates an overarching strategy—an understanding of what the company or enterprise wants to achieve and how marketing can help attain it—and a plan of attack for getting there. Products and services are only one part of the overall strategy.

A marketing plan that has reinvention as the strategic imperative should have key objectives and milestones that are measurable in both the short and long term. If metrics aren't part of the strategy, they should be added. Businesses need to see the short- and long-term return on investment they are getting from their marketing expenditures. These need to be hard measures, not soft—if a brand isn't selling, it's not succeeding. My experience in consumer, business-to-consumer, and business-to-business marketing proves this to be true.

Reinvention must be tied to brand positioning. *Brand* has become an overused word. There are consumer brands, business-to-consumer brands, business-to-business brands, lifestyle brands, and even personal brands—you name it, it has a brand. At its essence, a brand is a connection that results in perceptions and beliefs being held by and between two parties (such as a business and its customers). It's how the people your company or enterprise wants to do business with view your product or service. By not positioning a brand strategically, that connection can be at a minimum misunderstood, and at a maximum under-developed or even lost.

Brands need to be constantly reinvented to remain relevant, but that reinvention must be carefully and strategically under-taken. Before embarking upon such a path, marketing must understand how the brand is perceived today as well as how it will be perceived tomorrow and the day after that and the day after that.

Research remains a key part of marketing, but its applica-tion in this Internet-oriented world is different. It is as much about understanding perceptions as it is about understanding preferences. Those perceptions are crucial. With the rise in social media like Twitter, Facebook, and MySpace, a brand's image can be impacted immediately. One customer's bad expe-rience can turn into a public relations fiasco courtesy of an unflattering blog post or a single tweet. That is why both an understanding of the relevance of a brand's positioning and an understanding of the brand's perceptions are so important in this new landscape.

The Science of Marketing—Measurement

After defining the strategy that will guide the marketing approach, marketers must determine that the programs that bring the strategy to life are effective and cost-efficient. The only way to do that is through measurement. In today's data-driven, technology-oriented world, there is simply no excuse for not monitoring and rigorously evaluating return on investment.

Marketing has often been viewed as more of an art than a science. Historically, it's as if marketers were not really seen as businesspeople. In many cases this label was warranted, because many marketers fell into the following trap: it's more fun to be creative performers and magicians than it is to be num-ber crunchers and real businesspeople. However, if marketers are to prove their relevance and importance to a business or enterprise—and ensure that when times get hard, marketing dollars are increased to improve profitable sales that yield greater revenues instead of decimated to save dollars—they must focus on analysis and measurement.

When creating a strategic marketing plan, marketers must show projected metrics to prove each program's worth. And once these programs are approved and implemented, their outcomes must be measured to prove their effectiveness. If they are not effective—if they are not increasing profitable sales and driving revenue—they should, and must, be reinvented or eliminated.

Which again begs the question—how is marketing measured? Marketing is measured by delivering specific opportunities to increase your total return from marketing investments and through the provision of insights into how various marketing initiatives drive profitable sales and revenue growth.

At the program level, the first step is to perform a marketing analysis to measure incremental volume and return on investment for each tactical initiative or program that is undertaken. While this may seem as if a marketer is getting too deeply "into the weeds," it is imperative to understand the programs that work. A structured and comprehensive analysis will teach a number of lessons about a product or service's targets and buyers—most important, which of the various tools, techniques, campaigns, and programs work. Marketing can then look more deeply at the data to determine why one campaign or program worked and another didn't. With this information, marketers can revise their tactics and start all over again using the most effective methods—a never-ending but critically valuable process that must not only be encouraged but embraced as well.

Repeat and Repeat, Again and Again: Research

Research begins with the identification of a problem and formulation of a hypothetical solution to that problem. That solution is then tested and retested through further research. The design for the research is a framework or blueprint for conducting the marketing research project, and it involves the following steps that can and should be repeated in a changing environment:

1. Secondary data analysis
2. Qualitative research
3. Methods of collecting quantitative data (survey, observation, and experimentation)
4. Definition of the information needed
5. Measurement and scaling procedures
6. Questionnaire design
7. Sampling process and sample size
8. Plan of data analysis[2]

The research findings then help marketing better define and position the strategy, and they underpin planning, execution, and continual refinement of implementation plans. Notwithstanding the necessity of continuous learning, marketing has long suffered from the view that it is too wedded to research as opposed to real-world results. Today, on Twitter and Facebook as well as through other online communities, target consumers and customers are more than willing to provide feedback—they are built-in, continuously available focus and in-market trial groups. Marketing must reinvent its relationship with research, going from research as a driver to research as an ongoing element of strategy.

Understanding the Why

The key to improved performance is to debrief success as rigorously as failure. By so doing, marketing gains insight and perspective not only on the "what" of consumer or customer behavior, but also on the "why." By understanding the "why," a better, optimal, and ultimately more successful marketing mix can be created.

Terms like *marketing mix* harken back to art terminology. However, it's not. An effective marketing mix is based on data that demonstrates what tactic, campaign, or program grows profitable sales for, or raises interest in, a product or service. To optimize the marketing mix, marketing must run various scenarios to determine how to improve returns. By creating conservative, moderate, and aggressive growth scenarios to improve returns, marketing can respond (with some contractual limitations) immediately to what's happening in the market.

Determining return on marketing investment also includes having a marketing investment action plan. Marketers must be able to swiftly transfer funds to programs and tactics that improve the bottom line—and away from campaigns, programs, or initiatives that do not.

Now, that does not mean it is a good idea to flood the market with one type of marketing program. That can turn consumers or customers off as quickly as it attracted them in the first place. The objective is not to create a fad or overwhelm and saturate the prospect. Rather, the goal is to create a brand that impacts the market and brings dollars to the bottom line for a very long time.

When I was president of a leading marketing consulting firm, we worked with a number of beverage companies. At one time, we worked with a South American beverage company that spent more than $100 million on marketing across four countries. The company leaders had no idea what the company return on this investment was—they had never measured it. When they brought our consultancy in, the company's profits were shrinking, sales slowing—and a new competitor was poised to take advantage of the company's weakness. Once our consultants were able to understand and demonstrate the value of regional versus national marketing investments, which brands delivered the best returns, and the most effective media for investment, we were able to create and optimize a marketing mix for the company that provided the opportunity to improve marketing returns by approximately $9 million annually.

Creating Brands and Driving Revenue

Aren't profitable sales the true and ultimate determinant of marketing effectiveness? The simple answer is yes. However, marketers are not only focused on sales; they are also interested in creating, maintaining, and enhancing a brand's performance over time.

Brands, particularly those with a loyal fan base, drive dollars to the bottom line for years. Product sales may not matter, as depicted in the previous Pizza Hut anecdote: they may be commoditized and seen as no different from a competitor's version. If this happens, consumers or customers are being driven to shop on price. Remember the earlier tenet: consumers and customers are looking for value. Marketers want customers to value the brand so they will buy it at a premium, not only when it's on sale.

Take, as another example, milk. Shoppers will not normally pay a premium for milk, simply because, from their perspective, one type of milk is the same as any other. However, when it comes to beer, consumers tend to be brand loyal. One beer is not the same as another to the beer drinker, especially since the age of designer and microbrew beers began. Generally, the only time people will drink any brand of beer they are given is at ballparks or stadiums, where choice is relatively limited.

What's the difference between creating a brand and creating immediate sales? The difference is a marketing strategy that utilizes a new way of looking at marketing as well as metrics that measure the effectiveness of programs and plans. Otherwise there is the risk of creating a fad, like mood rings. Remember them? Every so often you hear about mood rings making a comeback—but then they disappear again. That type of selling doesn't have a long-term impact on the bottom line.

The Great Recession and Enduring Brand Loyalty

Has the recent recession killed brand loyalty? It's a question to ponder, as Americans' spendable discretionary cash has declined and price may have become the primary driver of purchases. However, I tend to agree with Steve Tobak's comment in the Corner Office blog: "Brand loyalty isn't dead. The concept still holds, still makes sense. But for products and services anybody really cares about—you're not talking detergent here—brand loyalty in the absence of differentiation, a value proposition that's consistently delivered upon, is definitely a thing of the past."[3]

Enduring brands can keep a company afloat during tough economic times or throughout transition periods and business cycles; that's why pharmaceutical companies fight so hard to keep their patents on the drugs they create. Brand loyalists want their initially doctor-prescribed medication and will ask pharmacists for it by name. However, once a patented medication ends, other forces such as insurance coverage and reduced price come into play. Take, for example, Lipitor, the cholesterol-fighting statin that is Pfizer's largest-selling brand. Once a generic version of the drug becomes available, currently scheduled for 2011, the price for Lipitor will inevitably drop, and health insurance companies may require patients to use the less expensive generic. That will cut deeply into Pfizer's bottom line. In fact, according to the *New York Times*, Pfizer has already started preparing for the loss of the patent by cutting the jobs of 800 researchers.[4] Similarly, Pfizer's Viagra is also soon coming off patent and going over-the-counter, and revenue declines of 70 to 85 percent can be expected based upon industry norms in the first year.

As further evidence of the critical loss of revenue from the expiring patents, in the fall of 2010, Pfizer reported that it would buy King Pharmaceuticals for $3.6 billion in cash, or $14.25 per share, a 40 percent premium over the stock's closing price. While the deal is subject to regulatory approval, Pfizer is seeking to facilitate, as part of the company's reinvention strategy, a revenue cushion for its patents that are set to expire in 2011.

Marketing Tools and Technology

Just as every other department within a company has technology tools that are specifically created to help them manage their processes and systems effectively and efficiently, so must marketers. An investment in this type of tool helps determine the means for creating a long-lasting bond with customers or consumers and therefore is imperative to the scientific side of marketing.

Marketers often tend to view technology as a tool to build sales, not as a tool to help them do their jobs better. However, many different technologies can help marketers increase the effectiveness of marketing programs. Marketers should add at a minimum the following technologies to their arsenal to achieve greater planning and process efficiencies, and enhanced resource deployment and return on marketing investment analytics:

>> Marketing planning tools
>> Marketing process management software
>> Digital asset and marketing resource management programs
>> Marketing tracking software

REMEMBER

- Analyze results of marketing programs.
- Use these insights to create a working hypothesis on how to reach your target audiences.
- Act on your learning to create a new, more effective marketing program.
- Measure and remeasure again and then again.
- Debrief success as rigorously as you debrief failure to understand both the "why" and the "what" of customer and consumer behavior.

Frameworks, Frameworks, Frameworks

Marketers must be globally consistent in their approach
to reinvention and marketing. Frameworks are the best
and most effective way of ensuring this mission can
be accomplished. They provide a consistent means for
locality-by-locality, state-by-state, country-by-country,
and region-by-region comparisons.

I am sure you have heard the phrase "It takes a village to raise a
child." It's a well-known adage that serves as the title or chapter of more than one book. Well, it also takes a village to create
a marketing initiative or campaign. Once that campaign is created, the village (global, regional, or national) has to execute
it—flawlessly, seamlessly, efficiently, and effectively. The key to
accomplishing these objectives is to create and deploy frameworks that everyone can follow, be they in Boston, Beijing,
Brussels, or Botswana.

What is a framework? It is, very simply, a template, guide, or
conceptual approach for creating a plan, developing a strategy,
conducting studies, approaching a problem, or reporting information that allows a company or enterprise to take a global strategy
to the local marketplace. (However, if there is not a global strategy, then there is no need for a global brand or to manage the
brand globally.)

Frameworks come in many guises: they are used for concepts,
taxonomy, research, execution, or financial documentation and

analytics. Frameworks need to be flexible so they can be customized to meet the needs of the local marketplace, yet they need to be rigid enough to ensure that the brand's essence remains sacrosanct. In this chapter, the focus is on those frameworks most commonly used by marketers to reinvent and manage a product or service.

Why Frameworks?

The use of frameworks provides discipline and commonality, something the field of marketing, often seen as an art, is sorely in need of if it hopes to be a key contributor to business in our data-intensive world and if it hopes to be globally consistent in its approach to the marketplace.

When I first joined KPMG as its vice chairman, marketing and communications, I asked to review the firm's U.S. marketing plan. There was none. Yes, some of the marketing and communications teams had created plans, but they were primarily tactical or product budget plans that were not aligned with the strategy of the industry, area, or service line being supported.

So one of my immediate priorities was to create a framework for the creation of marketing plans for this matrix-managed firm's five lines of business, three service lines, and six geographic areas, which at that time totaled more than $4.5 billion in annual revenue originating from 87 cities. I concurrently requested the creation of internal and external communications plans to parallel and integrate with the marketing plans.

These frameworks were built on the strategic operating plans developed at the firm, line of business, service line, and geographic area levels, as well as those created by individual local markets in cooperation with the marketing and communications team. As a result of these frameworks, the marketing team had a deep understanding of the firm's strategy and how our marketing goals fit into achieving that strategy.

Strategic Planning Frameworks

The most important framework from a marketing perspective is the framework for the strategic marketing plan. This plan must be based on the company or enterprise's overall strategic plan, taking into account the vision, goals, and plans of the company or enterprise. The overall strategic marketing plan is the template for the product or service plans that fall under marketing's purview.

As the foundation for all the plans to follow, the framework for a strategic marketing plan should include statements of the following:

>> Essence, defined as the core of the brand
>> Vision, defined as what the brand wants to be to its targets
>> Mission, simply meaning what attitudes or habits this product or service is going to change
>> Goals, which must be measurable
>> The plan to accomplish the goals, which should include
  > Products and services
  > Initiative or campaign tactics
  > Metrics
  > Research
>> The budget for product and service campaigns as well as for the overall organization

Budget Frameworks

Budget frameworks should at a minimum include the following organizational costs:

>> **Full-time employees (FTEs).** When computing this cost, include the total compensation cost—the cost of salary, benefits, and any projected bonus. It is only by including these expenses that the company or enterprise's and marketing's

leaders can understand the total cost of the organization to the company or enterprise.

» **Part-time employees and interns.** Often the cost of part-timers or interns is not factored in early enough in the planning. If you have truly thought through your marketing initiative or campaign, you should know what your people needs will be. If you cannot provide this cost, go back to the beginning to determine it.

» **Vendors/consultants.** Too often, I have been astonished by marketers that budget for vendors simply by adding 30 percent to the previously approved budgeted number they ended up spending last year. Consultants are not substitutes for full-time employees. They should be brought in for the experience or expertise that an organization does not and will not have. They should be used on specific projects that are budgeted for, and their costs should be rolled up to the top line as well as made plain in the initiative or campaign budget, and that budget should not be exceeded.

» **Administrative costs.** Lots of different things are hidden in administrative budgets, such as professional associations and training. These don't belong in an administrative budget: training should be a line item by itself, and professional association costs should be ascribed to the individual employee. Every administrative budget should have line items that roll up to the final number. Without that, an administrative budget should not be approved.

» **Technology.** The costs of technology are very rarely broken out in marketing budgets. However, the marketing department will generally make investments in technology, particularly in monitoring, the gathering of insights, and analytics-based tools. This investment needs to be broken out so that its return on investment can be measured.

» **Training.** It's true when they say that people are a company or enterprise's greatest asset. The creation of institutional knowledge and knowledge sharing is critical. It is a leader's responsibility to ensure that the company or enterprise commits to its growth by having a dedicated training or development budget. Managers, let alone marketers, must be committed to not only growing profitable sales, but to growing their team members' skills and encouraging their talents. Additionally, since technology changes so quickly, marketers must be kept up to speed on the latest advancements and developments so they can evaluate whether these technologies could make an impact on the way the company or enterprise goes to market.

Product or Service Frameworks

These plans need to be the most detailed, as they need to include the following:

» Goals, or simply what the plan will accomplish
» Strategy to achieve the goals
» Tactics, which should include a discussion of the following:
  › Audiences
  › Channels
  › Metrics
  › Resources
  › Budget per tactic

These frameworks should be used globally—literally meaning across the globe, in every country in which the company or enterprise is doing business, not simply across the national or domestic organization. Created correctly, frameworks can be localized or customized to the needs of a specific country related to channels or other elements of the marketing mix. At the end of the month or the end of a quarter, the head of a marketing department, CMO, CDO, or CEO should be able to look at consistent reporting against a series of metrics for all initiatives or campaigns.

That leads us to another type of framework every marketing department must have: a reporting framework.

Reporting Frameworks

Typically, every manager or executive has had to complete reports on progress against goals. Most of them are fairly innocuous. My personal "favorite" is the "Traffic Light" report, which uses red, yellow, and green lights as measures of whether a project is on track (green), in some trouble (yellow), or seriously off track (red). While this gives a manager an idea of progress, it doesn't give any reasons *why* a project is or is not on track, and it doesn't provide (or artfully avoids) metrics.

Actual, useful reporting needs to include the following:

» Campaign update, including tactics and channels utilized
» Key metrics, including impact to sales
» Resources utilized, including consultants
» Key learning, specifically what has worked, what doesn't work, and why

Remember, success must be debriefed as rigorously as failure—and it is imperative to share this learning across the organization.

The importance of frameworks cannot be overstated. They provide the outline of the business of marketing, and through analytics and metrics, they produce the data, insights, and conclusions that prove the value of marketing. Without frameworks, marketing reverts back to being an art—something soft and innocuous that can be questioned and cut, and something that can be applied differently by each practitioner.

Marketing and sales personnel tend to complain about reporting and frameworks. They feel that reporting takes them away from their focus on the consumer or customer and toward an internal focus. Nothing could be further from the truth. Metrics and ongoing research keep marketers and salespeople centered and constantly focused on their impact. If marketing cannot measure its impact, then it is failing at its job, because it is not driving profitable sales and growing revenues.

At the end of the day, remember, that is what marketers are here to do—drive profitable sales, increase market share, and build brands for the long term. Frameworks help you accomplish just that and should serve as a mandatory component of any company or enterprise embarking on reinvention.

Determining Success and Failure

Can frameworks be overdone? Of course they can. Many consulting firms are wedded to their frameworks at the expense of reality—let alone practicality. Many companies or enterprises have worked with consultants who come into their midst with binders of what they have done for other clients and promise to do the same for the current organization. And then they do exactly the same—even when the company or enterprise is in a different industry sector than the consultants' previous clients. Much of the data these consultants bring is prepopulated and based on where the company or enterprise has been, not where it is going. Most important, while such consultants don't listen to the client's current goals, they expect the company or enterprise's executives to listen to them since they are the experts.

Then the consultants depart, leaving behind binders that outline what they think the company or enterprise needs to do to succeed but include no roadmap to achieve success. They, more often than not, offer no implementation guide or metrics for success. Rather, they provide a strategy . . . and they leave. In these consultants' view, if the strategy succeeds, it's because of the consultants' work . . . and if it fails, it's because the company or enterprise didn't hew to their strategy.

That is where consultative frameworks fail.

Frameworks succeed when they are used to measure progress and hold marketers accountable for results. They must be flexible enough to encompass geographical differences, but strong and robust enough that marketing has an accurate view of overall budget expenditures.

One of the biggest misperceptions about marketing is that the funds assigned to marketing go into a "black hole." With frameworks, marketers not only prove this is a misconception but can provide an accurate view of what channels work and what don't for the targeted audiences. This is vital as the marketing plan goes forward because budgets must be flexible enough to allow for shifting and migration of dollars over time to the tactics that drive profitable sales, grow revenues, and attract new customers while keeping longtime loyalists.

At the end of the day, that is the true measure of a marketer's worth. And the proper frameworks allow a marketer to prove that worth, at any point in time, to anyone who asks.

REMEMBER

- Frameworks take the reinvention conceived as a global strategy to the local marketplaces.
- Frameworks allow for budgetary oversight and provide a means of country-to-country and region-to-region comparisons.
- Frameworks provide consistency and commonality of reporting, measurement, and approach to issues and problems.
- Frameworks afford a means for determining which channels work and which don't, and they should be flexible enough to allow for transfer of resources to those that do.
- Frameworks can be localized without losing the integrity of the reporting model.

Perception Really Is Your Customer's Reality

Reinvention requires reinventing the relationship with the customer so that the experience itself has value. How we interact with prospects and customers determines how we are perceived, and perception, in reality, is reality.

F rameworks prove the impact of marketing internally. But the ultimate focus of the marketer must always be external, on the customer or prospect. In the age of the Internet and the resultant proliferation of channels of communication, there may be no more important driver of ongoing repeat purchase or proxy for long-term success for a company or enterprise than a customer service evaluation. Increasingly, the one area that has a wholly disproportionate impact on ratings and on predisposing potential customers is social media. To paraphrase Amazon .com's Jeff Bezos, in the days of brick and mortar stores, a bad experience meant a customer told six friends. In this age of Facebooking and blogging, dissatisfied customers now can tell six million or more. And they can keep telling their stories over and over, time and time again.

Given this new reality, and knowing that marketers are not simply creating, promoting, or selling a product or service once, but rather creating an all-encompassing brand experience that drives customer loyalty and repeat sales, you would think in today's Internet-oriented world there would be an intense focus by business managers on customer service and the customer experience. That, more often than not, however, is not the reality.

Quite simply, customer service is paramount to the brand experience. More important, customer facing representatives are not only on the front line—they are often the single most memorable experience a prospect or a customer has with the company or enterprise, both before and after the purchase. As a result, the interaction between customer service and the customer or consumer must epitomize the type of relationship marketers want to create for the brand.

Ideally, every interaction should leave a customer or consumer wanting to tell others about his or her experience. All customer interactions should be positive, proactive, nonevasive, nonadversarial, responsive, and oriented to solving a problem if one exists. Unfortunately, such interactions are typically not most people's experience—and it's no surprise that so many brand stories tell and retell the tale of bad customer service experiences.

The Comcast Experience

The poster child for bad customer service has for many years been the cable television industry. And the worst of the worst in the public perception has long been Comcast, which was founded in 1963 as a single-system cable operation. Today, Comcast is the country's largest provider of cable services, and one of the world's leading communications companies. Yet, not surprisingly, when you "Google" Comcast, "Comcast customer service" comes up as the second most frequent search term, after "Comcast.net."

Generally, very few consumers are satisfied with, let alone like, their cable company, but the vitriol directed at Comcast by consumers is, perhaps as posited previously, the worst of the bunch. One video on YouTube pays "tribute" to Comcast service, and not in a positive light. Called "A Comcast Technician Sleeping on my Couch,"[1] the video shows this particular technician asleep in a customer's house and states in considerable detail how the technician, a Comcast employee, was on hold for more than an hour with headquarters before he fell asleep. That video has, as of this writing, more than 1.5 million viewings on YouTube, and it went viral when it was first posted, going from e-mail to e-mail around the globe.

If this were a one-time occurrence, people would laugh and probably dismiss it. However, it isn't. In fact, *Time* magazine provides further legitimacy and authenticity by calling Comcast "perhaps the most frustrating pay TV provider in a world of pay TV providers driving consumers bonkers."[2] And, it's not the only one to shine a negative spotlight on the company, as The Consumerist, a consumer issues website, bestowed upon Comcast its "Worst Company in America" award.[3]

Why? Well, add the YouTube video to this earlier brand legacy of Comcast, cited by the Associated Press:

> Like most everybody, LaChania Govan got bounced around when she called her cable company to complain. She made dozens of calls and was even transferred to a person who spoke Spanish—a language she doesn't understand. But when she got her August bill from Comcast she had no trouble understanding she'd made somebody mad. It was addressed to "Bitch Dog." . . . Two employees were fired after company officials went through records and identified them as being involved in the incident.[4]

These types of stories about Comcast are legion and have given rise to what is now seen by many in the marketplace as an urban truth—that Comcast keeps a list of customers who complain too much, and those customers get their services cut and get hung up on when they call. True or not, it is part of the Comcast mythos. As a result of such beliefs, and further corroborated by other true-life experiences, there is a website dedicated to Comcast's customer services issues, simply called comcast sucks.org.

Comcast is determined to change that image. In fact, Rick Germano, when he was first named senior vice president for customer operations, said that customers had told him that "Most of all, they want us to show up when we say we will and get the job done right the first time."[5]

The problem is—from a brand perspective, isn't that the least a customer should expect?

To underscore its "new" commitment, Comcast has made the promise of dramatically improved customer service one of the key messages of its advertising. In fact, its website today says, "We want our customers to be amazed with the choice Comcast offers, excited by the innovation Comcast provides and satisfied with the service and reliability of every interaction with Comcast."[6]

How can there be such a wide divergence of views between how its customers see the service they receive and how the company sees the service it provides? After all, the perceived flaws in the company's service (as well as the service of its competitors) have taken such a root in the public consciousness that *Advertising Age* once suggested the company spend its money on improving customer service instead of advertising.[7]

The bottom line is that every time a customer has a bad experience with a brand, the brand is damaged. And the bottom line—financial performance—takes the real hit. The result for Comcast could be that additional services are not purchased. New services are not added. On-demand movies are not purchased. Revenue opportunities are lost, and even worse, customers close their accounts and choose alternative providers such as DIRECTV or DISH Network satellite TV.

Why Customer Satisfaction Isn't Job One

Astonishingly, customer service continues to get short shrift from many if not most companies. It's not central to their brand strategy and their thinking about their customers and prospects. James Surowiecki summed up the bottom line well in a piece for the *New Yorker* when he wrote:

> Customer service is a classic example of what businessmen call a "cost center"—a division that piles up expenses without bringing in revenue—and most companies see it as tangential to their core business, something they have to do rather than

something they want to do. Although some unhappy customers complain, most don't—one study suggests that only six percent of dissatisfied customers file a complaint—and it's tricky to quantify the impact of good service.[8]

Customer service is many things—a creator of relationships with the consumer and a means of learning how a product relates and interacts with the audience, to name but two—but it is not a cost center.

Americans are savvy and vocal consumers. When they have an issue with a product or service, they complain—not only to the company, but to their friends. Companies that take the customer service relationship for granted—as Dell did, for example—lose both the consumers' loyalty and their willingness to try or purchase a new product. Bad customer service can very easily outshine a good product, as anyone who has endured a scripted conversation with a call center rep can attest. So, is customer service a cost center? Not at all. Customer service representatives are, first and foremost, brand ambassadors. Their effect may be hard to quantify, but it's real, and it makes a difference to the bottom line.

The Profit Impact of Good Service

Apple understands the criticality of the customer experience. Many other companies don't sufficiently internalize the understanding that the brand experience is part and parcel of the customer experience, and the customer experience doesn't stop with the sale. The sale is only the beginning. Apple's management truly gets it. That's why, for the seventh year in a row, Apple topped the University of Michigan's American Customer Satisfaction Index (ACSI), achieving a score of 86 out of 100.[9]

Apple is a shining example of a company that doesn't view customer service as a cost center. Rather, Apple considers customer service an important part of a larger experience—the brand experience. This is one key to reinvention: see the parts of marketing not as separate, but as part of a whole creating an overall experience for the customer—one the customer will constantly want to repeat. It certainly makes a difference, as the Cult of Mac website confirms:

> Apple is dominating its competition in customer service because the company cares about creating a quality customer experience at every brand touch point. And they do this for a reason—it's called "profit." Apple has built an immensely successful business model around the depth of caring about product experience, and it's translating all the way from customer sentiment to Wall Street. From corporate leadership and the vision of Steve Jobs to customized retail environments showcasing flawless product design, Apple is invested in delivering amazing experiences to their customers.[10]

The Importance of Follow-On Sales

So, why aren't all companies focusing on the total customer experience, starting with customer service? And why aren't marketers leading the reinvention of customer service to drive revenue and follow-on sales that take place after the initial purchase of a product or service? The *New Yorker* captures the reason very clearly:

> The real problem may be that companies have a roving eye: they're always more interested in the customers they don't have. So they pour money into sales and marketing to lure new customers while giving their existing ones short shrift, in an effort to minimize costs and maximize revenue. Then, once they've got us, their attention wanders.[11]

Marketers often seem to want only what they do not already have. That is why reinvention that focuses on the buyer is so important. By focusing on the essence of the product or service, a marketer is forced to identify the target audience. These are the customers or consumers who will not only try the brand, but will stay with it and advocate for it—no matter the price. These are the people who drive profit and create return business—the brand loyalists.

Attracting new sales and gaining new customers can drive profits in the short term. But will the entire experience make those consumers and customers brand loyalists? Not until customer service is reinvented and the experience itself has value.

Reinventing a Customer's Relationship by Putting the Customer First

Nordstrom's has as its cornerstone a commitment to customer service—a dedication that remains unchanged after more than 100 years in the retailing industry. In fact, a book has been written about Nordstrom's customer service—*The Nordstrom Way: The Inside Story of America's #1 Customer Service Company* by Robert Spector and Patrick D. McCarthy.[12] One of the key components of Nordstrom's customer philosophy is that employees are instructed to always make a decision that favors the customer before the company. They are never criticized for doing too much for a customer; they are criticized for doing too little.

As a result, it's not unusual for a department manager to continue to serve a former client as a salesperson or personal shopper after a promotion or even when the manager no longer works in the particular department where the client is buying. What a concept—the client is important above all else.

When was the last time you heard about a company criticizing its employees for doing too little for the customer? It's so rare as to be almost unknown. Yet one of the keys to a brand's core is the emotional connection between the product or service and the people who purchase it—reinforced by their experience with brand ambassadors such as sales personnel and customer service representatives. Good customer service builds that connection. Jay Goltz blogged the following for the *New York Times*:

When you walk into a store, and there is virtually no help, it's because someone figured out that the company could save X dollars if it cut back the labor budget by 7 percent. When you walk out disgusted and sales go down, the store blames it on the economy or brutal competition.[13]

Goltz is correct. Too many companies fail to look in the mirror. Nor do they reconsider and reprioritize their investments to reflect all the many facets of the brand experience, including customer service.

We have talked a great deal about core essence. Essential to that is the relationship with the customer—not simply the transactional relationship, but the ongoing, mature relationship, from cradle to grave. Think of Apple, once again. Its fall 2010 commercial for the then-new iPhone shows a new father showing a new grandfather the first pictures of his new baby. That's the Apple philosophy encapsulated in very personal terms: the customer experience is primary—and generationally long lasting.

REMEMBER

- Reinvention means reinventing the relationship with the customer. How we interact with the buyers of our products and services determines, in large part, how a brand is perceived in the marketplace. And the overall brand experience is what makes that perception a reality.
- Changing a brand's name doesn't change the customer's brand experience. And customers have long memories—and, with the Internet, a large megaphone.
- While brand architecture gives consumers or customers reasons for buying a product or service, the customer experience coupled with the actual product or service experience is what creates brand loyalty.
- Brand loyalty and the repeat purchase of a product or service drives increased revenues for the long term—that's the essence of creating a complete (and some might call it "virtuous") brand experience.

Communicate;
Then Communicate
Some More

As a marketer or communicator, it is your responsibility
to keep messages clear, concise, and, most important,
consistent. Marketing must then communicate these
reinvention-laden messages in as many different ways
through as many different channels as it takes to effectively
and efficiently reach the target audience—again and again.

C ommunications, to be effective, must begin with believabil-
ity and end with trust. This is where a brand's credibility
originates. Your brand's core essence must be credible; if it's
not, go back and reinvent it.

The Power of Communications

Perceptions are built on interactions, exchanges, and exposure
to communications. People, in turn, communicate their own
experiences with a brand through a variety of media. And in
today's world, that communication—that dissemination—is all
but instantaneous.

Marketing communications have long been undervalued, but
in fact, they are a critical part of any plan. Today, there is much
talk about "reputation management" communications. In fact,

this is simply another way of saying brand management communications. A company's reputation is distilled from its actions, its interactions, and its brand.

As an example there is, once again, Goldman Sachs, the renowned financial institution that has long envisioned itself as the master of the "masters of the universe" that run Wall Street. As seen during the recent financial crisis, that almost superior attitude seems to have created a tin—if not totally deaf—ear among its leadership, one of whom referred to what they do as "God's work," not recognizing that this work—rightly or wrongly—was viewed by many as costing more than 10 million people their jobs.

This recent high-profile affair demonstrated two truths of the new world order—the lightning speed of communications and the importance of managing perceptions. As a result of its inability to recognize the immediacy of the marketplace and its lack of understanding of the importance of nuanced communications, Goldman Sachs damaged its brand—if not for the long term, certainly for the short term. So much so that when Goldman was indicted by the SEC in April 2010 for supposedly playing both sides of the mortgage crisis, betting against its clients, and profiting from the housing collapse, the *New York Times* said, "The accusations amount to a black eye for the once-untouchable Goldman Sachs, a money machine that is the epicenter of Wall Street power. For decades, its platinum reputation has attracted top investors and stock underwriting deals. . . . In recent months, Goldman has been defiant in the face of criticism, repeatedly defending its actions in the mortgage market, including its own bets against it."[1]

A company or enterprise underleverages its ability to create a pervasive brand when it undervalues communications and assumes indifference or, even worse, arrogance as its public face. What a company or enterprise says is now spread through so many channels that by not tying its marketing to its communications (and vice versa), a business enterprise can lose control of its brand and its reputation almost overnight.

Ensuring that messages around a brand are clear, sharp, consistent, and simple helps break through the clutter directly to the intended recipient of the communication. And the messages need to be constantly reinforced in different ways. Most important, messaging cannot change every day, though how messages are presented to various audiences and constituencies can and should.

Take Geico, the Berkshire Hathaway–owned insurance company. Its commercials use the gecko, the cavemen, a pair of googly eyes on a stack of dollars, and various celebrities, all to get across the message that "15 minutes can save you 15 percent or more on your insurance." Each ad either appeals to a different audience or simply utilizes a different creative execution to reinforce the same clear and simple idea.

Geico understands the value of a simple, clear, consistent message that is continuously leveraged in unique ways to reinforce its positioning and brand promise, without confusion about what the brand stands for and why it is needed. At the end of the day, such consistent messaging drives desire—desire to own, participate, collaborate, benefit, or purchase as well as to be part of an experience unlike that of the competition.

The Stumble of a Corporate Icon: Johnson & Johnson

In 1982, in a now well-known act of corporate responsibility, Johnson & Johnson recalled all of its Tylenol from U.S. store shelves six days after capsules tampered with in Chicago were linked to six fatalities. It was a gutsy, widely lauded move by the CEO that cost the company $100 million and almost destroyed its leading share of the market. However, consumers were impressed by the company's care for its buyers and, in a show of loyalty, sales rebounded within a year.

Unfortunately, Johnson & Johnson did not react as well for a more recent recall. In January 2010 the company began recalling Benadryl, Motrin, and Rolaids as users complained of nausea and other side effects. The time from the initial reports to the company's action? Twenty months—and it only happened after the Food and Drug Administration (FDA) forced the company to act, a very different circumstance from 1982. The media response was critical, as in this comment from the *Christian Science Monitor*:

> It's sad to see a corporate icon stumble, especially when the problems are of its own making. The move is a reminder of how fragile corporate reputations are.[2]

The incident not only hurt Johnson & Johnson's corporate reputation, it also affected the company's relationship with its regulator, the FDA. (What made matters even worse was that there were more recalls to come across a variety of product lines, various factories, and numerous business units that have continued into 2011.) Over the next four months, the company's business unit, McNeil Consumer Healthcare, had to announce some of these recalls to an increasingly unforgiving public. This opened McNeil to FDA criticism, with the group's press officer stating that "their initial response was unsatisfactory" after his group "repeatedly pressed them."[3]

Media criticism of parent company Johnson & Johnson grew as well, with Dailyfinance.com noting that "If the company can't regain parents' trust, the handling of this recall could send the company's reputation—and eventually its revenue from Tylenol—to the ground."[4]

As a result of this and other experiences on behalf of clients' mishandling of troubled brands, communications are one of my hot-button issues. It is my contention that marketing and communications departments should always be one combined organization, including public relations, human resource communications, executive communications, corporate social responsibility communications, and brand communications— any type of communications. This allows one team to be responsible internally for making employees the company or enterprise's best brand ambassadors and externally for communicating the brand to important constituencies—ensuring consistency in all messaging.

Unorthodox? Controversial for communications professionals? Perhaps. However, if communications are done correctly, they are built on brand positioning, as are all marketing activities.

And if communications are not handled properly, these activities can damage the brand overnight.

The Global Community—24/7

Technology has created a global community that in today's world is inextricably intertwined—24 hours a day, seven days a week. As a result, marketing and communications must work seamlessly together. The disciplines must interact consistently and continuously throughout each and every day to ensure that the brand's positioning, reputation, and messaging are synchronized and presented to its audiences clearly and concisely.

That, in a nutshell, is my argument for marketing and communications being combined in one team. In this around-the-clock, technologically driven world, they cannot exist separately and expect to succeed in offering an effective, consistent, and optimized brand message that must be delivered immediately to the marketplace.

A company or enterprise's reputation is distilled from its brand. A company's and a brand's reputation is based on the perceptions and interactions of consumers, customers, and other constituencies with all facets of the company or enterprise. These perceptions are based on the company's products and services, its brand positioning, its interaction with consumers and customers, and its portrayal in various media. In short, a reputation is built on how a brand's core essence is communicated and experienced.

Communications: The Toyota Trap

Toyota, the Japanese carmaker, has long been known as responsive to its owners and dealers. As a result, it had earned tremendous brand loyalty. However, when the company had problems related to its accelerators in the winter of 2009, it suddenly seemed to develop an inability to communicate—and as detailed earlier, it stonewalled.

Despite having warned its dealers as early as 2007 of the floor mat risk,[5] Toyota went dark publicly. Its subsequent reaction was to blame the media, saying the problem was not as widespread as was being reported. Then, as stories of people being endangered or killed as a result of accelerator pedals sticking started showing up on the news, Toyota said it was the customers' fault. Finally, appearing before a congressional committee, Toyota leaders said that there was no problem with its cars' electronics, it was simply a floor mat issue. U.S. Transportation Secretary Ray LaHood said in February 2010, "While Toyota is taking responsible action now, it unfortunately took an enormous effort to get to this point."[6]

It just kept getting worse and worse for Toyota, despite a recall and a staged apology from its CEO. As a result of its lack of forthright and transparent communications, Toyota sales fell in the United States following this negative portrayal in the media— even after offering significant incentives to potential buyers. The company was fined more than $16 million for its failure to notify the government in a timely manner about the issues it was having with gas pedals. But that wasn't the end of it for Toyota. In late December 2010, the Department of Transportation announced that the company had agreed to pay an additional $32.4 million in fines[7] (the maximum amount allowed by law) to settle two other Department of Transportation investigations. And finally, in late February 2011, the once proud brand announced that 2.17 million vehicles would be recalled to remedy mechanical flaws that could cause them to rush out of control.

Toyota learned its lesson the hard way. Consumer advocates and frightened owners of Toyota cars used the various communications channels available to them—cable news, blogs, social networks, and so on—to get out the story of the sticking pedals. This is the double-edged sword the Internet presents to companies. The company or enterprise cannot control the message. And if a company or enterprise is undergoing a crisis, these communications channels can turn and be used against it.

Very simply, it is not only the cable channels that offer news 24/7, it is also the social networking sites. One ill-considered pronouncement is bounced around the world in seconds. And reaction is just as fast.

From Respected Leader to Notorious Villain

Take, for another example, the recent issues in the financial services industry, particularly Bank of America. Originally founded in San Francisco, the Bank of America (B of A) brand was based on good customer relations and strong community ties.

As the banking industry consolidated and B of A became a global bank, that brand positioning was stretched, but it did not break—until the Great Recession, that is. Going into the recession, Bank of America was in a fairly strong position: it had cash and was growing. As the financial markets began to freeze and the impact of the recession began to be felt, the government reached out to Bank of America to help save Wall Street firms that it viewed as "too big to fail"—first Lehman Brothers, then Merrill Lynch.

When B of A didn't buy Lehman, the stalwart investment banking firm went under. Seeing the markets' reaction, the government aggressively encouraged—some would say pushed—B of A to consummate the Merrill Lynch deal. B of A was a hero, and it was able to grow into investment banking, something it had long wanted to do. Unfortunately, as the *New York Times* reported, the merger soured as the value of the combined companies plummeted from about $176 billion to a "market capitalization of only $39 billion."[8]

And then B of A faced a new problem with Merrill: the bonus issue. Agreements were made between B of A and Merrill concerning bonuses, but as public scrutiny bore down on the company, the issue spun out of control with no solution in sight. Not only was B of A pilloried publicly; internally, it faced lowering morale as a result of the merger as its employees blamed management for the eventual loss of their bonuses.[9]

Bank of America still hasn't recovered from the communications fiasco of the Merrill Lynch merger (and the subprime mortgage debacle of Countrywide Financial). Once again, hubris—company leaders' belief that bonuses were an internal issue, despite the company taking money from American taxpayers through the government's bailout of the banking industry—got in the way of a good and effective communications strategy.

REMEMBER

- Communications are consistently undervalued in marketing. However, they can and do impact the ability to reinvent a brand.
- Marketing and communications must be aligned, since they both have to do with managing a brand's reputation.
- In a crisis, consistent and immediate communications are key. Marketing and communications must work together to develop messaging so that sales don't suffer.
- The best brand ambassadors are a company's employees. Therefore, clearly communicate the brand to all employees so that they can explain it to others.

It's More than Just Channel Surfing

Communications channels have proliferated in the Internet era, but that doesn't mean that all channels should be used. Strategically review the available channels to determine which ones your brand's target audience uses, and exploit these to ensure successful reinvention and better return on investment.

Technology is responsible for many things—the increasing homogenization of culture, ease and immediacy of communications, global positioning systems, and so much more. The list goes on and on. From a marketing perspective, one of the benefits that digital technology has delivered to the marketplace is the overwhelming number and variety of channels available to get out marketing, sales, and public relations messages about a company or enterprise's products and services.

This chapter, however, is not about channel marketing; rather, it focuses on communications channels—the range of media available to speak directly to the target audience. Channel marketing means directing specific promotional efforts at specific links or levels in a channel of distribution (distributor, wholesaler, or retailer). The selection of channels and pricing always comes after positioning is determined. Nonetheless, they are not central to the reinvention of a company or enterprise—although they are very important to effective go-to-market selling efforts.

Communications Channels

One way of differentiating a brand and optimizing profitable sales is by the variety of channels marketers choose to reach a customer or consumer. The channel itself can communicate much about the brand.

When determining the proper channels to market a product or service, marketers begin with brand positioning and carefully selected target audiences. Marketers sometimes make assumptions about the channels that should be utilized or leveraged based on what is believed rather than factually known to be true about the actual actions of the target audiences, as discussed in Principle #10. In this era when technology changes frequently, new channels proliferate endlessly, and the recession has changed habits, any assumption can be an unforgiving mistake.

Before determining which channels are best for the reinvention of a particular product or service, marketers must learn at a minimum the following about their audience:

>> Key influencers
>> Means of communication
>> Technology utilized
>> Household demographics
>> Type of buyer (for example, impulse or comparison buyers)

Reinvention requires that marketers understand—not only intuitively but also with hard facts and figures—who the key influencers are and what they use to communicate. In the new age of marketing, marketers must understand how their messages, executions, offers, and incentives are best received (via advertising, in print, direct mail, e-mail, smartphone, or other means) and acted upon, not only how they are communicated.

Determining Channels

With this type of information, marketers may then begin to evaluate and determine the channels that strategically fit with and suit their product or service (much like a holistic ecosystem).

Let's look at Red Bull, one of the most strategically marketed product introductions of the recent past. Red Bull is an adaptation of the Thai energy drink Krating Daeng, which literally means "Red Bull." Now the market leader, Red Bull began its life in the Western world as a college campus phenomenon. Few people need the ability to stay up late and study (or socialize) as much as do college students—and the energy drink fit this lifestyle.

In the past few years, Red Bull has used its marketing resources to sponsor extreme sports—kayaking, wakeboarding, cliff-diving, surfing, skating, and freestyle motocross, to name a few—which appeal to its target demographic. In fact, Red Bull's introduction was one of the first viral marketing campaigns. It initially spread to clubs and other places younger people gathered. It then spread to celebrities—who, in at least this instance, did not look for recompense for using the product.

Early on, Red Bull did very little advertising via traditional media. It knew its target and knew the channels to leverage to reach its audience most effectively: clubs, college campuses, and extreme sports sponsorships. As Red Bull matured, it moved into more traditional media channels—television and print advertising.

Significantly, as it moved into new channels, Red Bull suffered no diffusion in its brand positioning. Brand diffusion can happen to any brand. Given the proliferation of channels, if outreach is not astutely managed, a product or service can lose its center and work against its core essence, positioning, and attributes. To avoid that mistake, it is imperative that marketers truly understand the many different aspects of their brand and leverage these different facets in various channels.

The Geek Squad as a Communications Channel

Another example of this is Best Buy stores. From a retail perspective, Best Buy is simply a big box store where consumers can purchase any and all types of electronics and technology, ranging from CDs and DVDs to large-screen high-definition televisions to computers and e-book readers. From a customer service perspective, Best Buy offers the Geek Squad. Best Buy uses the Geek Squad as a communications channel through which it makes its customer service focus credible and sustainable—two core elements of brand attributes.

Originally conceived as a means of offering help to the technology challenged consumer, Best Buy bought the Geek Squad and now offers it as an ancillary for-pay service to all consumers. According to the *Richmond Times-Dispatch*:

> About 24,000 "agents" worldwide come to work each day dressed in white button-down shirts, black pants and clip-on ties. They still make house calls in iconic black-and-white "Geekmobiles," and they are set up in all of Best Buy's 1,143 U.S. stores.[1]

Piper Jaffray analyst Mitch Kaiser perfectly summed up the Geek Squad's impact on the electronic store landscape:

> Geek Squad's going to become a bigger and bigger component of their core strategy. . . . Beyond driving sales, it increases customer satisfaction. Best Buy becomes the trusted adviser and the IT staff for the individual.[2]

Leveraging the New Technology Channels

Today, new channels are popping up almost daily, and these new channels even help determine the winners and losers in U.S. politics. Regardless of party affiliation, politics is all about marketing—marketing an idea, a reaction to the idea, a candidate, or a party. In the most recent presidential election it was the Democratic Party and the candidate's team marketing Barack Obama for president. Obama's core essence was "change": he said he could change Washington, D.C. His promise was "Yes We Can." He used a previously unexploited channel, "netroots" (Internet grassroots including social networks, wikis, and blogs), to reach people who previously were disenfranchised or uninterested in the political process and to bring these new people into his campaign. These were his targets: people who needed to believe that by engaging, they could make a difference.

National Public Radio called the elements of Obama's campaign "unprecedented in presidential politics" and provided a detailed look at his alliance:

> The organization has two crown jewels. One is a database with 13 million e-mail addresses. While some of them are bogus or came from non supporters (such as journalists covering the campaign), probably 10 million or more came from supporters—those who helped build the campaign's historic war chest, who organized in counties and precincts, or who simply attended a rally or bought a T-shirt. The other jewel is the "net roots" style network that turned out voters for Obama in the primaries and that helped him carry traditionally Republican states in November."[3]

The Democratic candidate raised enormous sums of money using these "netroots" to reach those who believed in his promise of change. Once in power, however, governing replaced rhetoric. The netroots list was turned over to the Democratic National Committee to be used in traditional means of raising money, and change was replaced by compromise. And the Democrats returned to traditional channels to reach the populace—town hall meetings, speeches, news conferences, and so on. The Internet-savvy team took a step away from their technology (in fact, Robert Gibbs didn't get on Twitter until more than a year after the president was elected; David Axelrod, the president's key communications aide, still isn't on Twitter as of this writing), despite the fact that the president refused to give up his BlackBerry.

Consequently, President Obama experienced erosion in his populist base, which affected how every Democrat running for office marketed himself or herself in the following midterm election, one that was viewed as a "tsunami" for the Democrats, who lost their majority position in the House of Representatives and came very close to losing their majority in the Senate. How that will play out will be seen over the next few years. As of mid-2010, according to the Associated Press, "49 percent of people now approve of the job Obama is doing—and only 44 percent like how he has handled health care and the economy."[4]

A side note: this disillusion with the president and his policies gave impetus to the rise of the Tea Party movement. The foundation and the future of the Tea Party are still being written, but with Sarah Palin, a possible 2012 Republican presidential candidate, as one of its titular leaders, it cannot be sloughed off as the Know-Nothings of the 21st century. The Tea Party may change the face of the Republican Party, taking it back to its conservative fiscal roots. It's an interesting time for a party that campaigns extremely and, in the past, has governed moderately (remember, it was the Bush administration, when Republicans controlled both the House and the Senate, that passed and signed into law the bailout of financial institutions that is detested by the Tea Party). Will the Tea Party be responsible for taking the Republicans back to their economic core? This is an interesting question whose answer remains to be seen.

Channels Can Make or Break a Product or Service

Sarah Palin first used the term *death squad* in relation to health-care reform legislation on her Facebook page.[5] Gavin Newsom, the mayor of San Francisco, officially announced he was running for Senate from California on Twitter.[6] In both cases, social media was the channel chosen by these politicians to reach their constituents.

The channels chosen for reinvention can make a product or service—or break it. That is why up-front comprehensive research is extremely important. Marketers must know their audience as well as they know their brand and then identify and effectively exploit the channels that are used by and important to these target audiences.

The channels chosen should strengthen, not weaken, a brand's positioning. Always be aware of the nontraditional channels— the "netroots," if you will. For a product launch, sometimes a viral campaign is more important than a celebrity endorsement.

And sometimes it's all about the promotion or endorsement—or no endorsement at all. In Delaware, Christine O'Donnell, the Tea Party candidate, won the Republican Party's nomination for Senate without the support of mainstream Republicans, but with that of Sarah Palin. While she lost the general election, her upset primary victory sent a message to Republicans that their party did not control the Tea Party; rather the Tea Party was to be taken seriously.

Determining whether or not a channel is working requires metrics. The return on investment in a channel must be measured, be it in the number of online hits, calls to and conversions from an 800-number, "buzz" in blogs or on Twitter, responses to advertising, or other action. However, in the end, the final determinant will be profitable sales and growing revenues. Marketers will know they are using the right channels if a product or service attracts the target audience—and they buy.

REMEMBER

- Know the digital channels the target audience uses and target the investment for reinvention there.
- Keep abreast of new and diverse channels.
- Don't use a scattershot approach to channels—it will only dilute the brand's messages.
- Differentiate the brand not only by how it is positioned, but also by how it is communicated.
- Use consistent and repetitive messages derived from the brand's positioning and its architecture in all targeted channels.

DO THE RIGHT THINGS FOR THE RIGHT REASONS

MANY BUSINESSES and even more marketers today believe they are missing out if they aren't on Facebook, Twitter, or similar sites or applications where communities of consumers gather and congregate. However, reinvention requires doing what is best for the brand and not falling prey to the tendency and pressure to do what everyone else is doing. That is especially true when it comes to social networking.

If it doesn't make sense for your brand to have on online presence based on its essence and its audience, then don't do it. A marketer's job is to drive ever-increasing profitable sales. If an online social network presence isn't central to accomplishing that objective, then resist the pressure. Take the path of greater resistance, be it partnerships, celebrity endorsements, or relationships with regulators.

Do the right things for the right reasons—activities that effectively and efficiently accomplish growth as well as driving profitable sales, increased penetration, and greater market share.

It's All About
the Relationship

Social networks are not the be-all and end-all for
marketers undertaking a reinvention initiative. Don't
waste time or money marketing through a social network
unless marketing has the research and metrics that
justify its use and evidence that it drives profitable sales.

Ever wonder where "marketing" began? Once, when having
this conversation with a colleague, she told me (somewhat
parochially) that she had always believed that it started in
the United States in the general stores of early America. There,
the shopkeeper, in an attempt to reinvent the store's relationship
with a possible buyer, had to convince his or her customers of
the efficacy of a product when they had little money and the pro-
prietor had little supply. Not doing so could mean the difference
between survival and going out of business for the shop and its
owner in the long term, as well for its suppliers. Shopkeepers had
to know their customers and prospects, know their town, and
know their environment to market products and services under
those circumstances.

While the global community would have much to say about
such a provincial view of marketing, it is clear that marketing
from the beginning has been about the connection between a
product or service and the person buying it. It's about loyalty,
value, and preference.

The Debate: Thumbs Up or Down

That is why I generally don't believe in the power or effectiveness of social networks in marketing products or services. Very simply, a long-term relationship between a product or service and a consumer or future customer generally cannot be currently created online via a community site. At best it is a matter of product or service impressions.

For any product or service to succeed in the marketplace, while it may be introduced online, it cannot be sustained over time without creating an intimate and firsthand personal relationship with the audience through the act of acquisition (or purchase). Audience members need ultimately to see it, feel it, taste it, or try it on (if it's a consumer product) or see and experience its actual benefits to them (if it's a service).

Many colleagues don't share this longer-term perspective. Yet no one has the ultimate answer. Brian Morrissey responded critically in *Brandweek*, noting:

> For all the excitement about social media, there's a specter hanging over its use by companies. Will all this Tweeting, blogging, and Facebooking pay off? For some proponents, the question is irrelevant. They agree with the view encapsulated in the social media bible *The Cluetrain Manifesto*—Markets are conversations. Companies have to participate in the conversations where they're happening, ROI be damned. Their dismissal of metrics is summed up in an oft-repeated question, "What's the ROI of putting on your pants on in the morning?"
>
> Those kind of pithy ripostes are music to the ears of the social-media faithful at conferences and on blogs, but they're unlikely to impress budget-constrained CMOs or CDOs who, while eager to find new ways to reach consumers and customers, are under more pressure to prove their efforts are pushing and moving the business forward. Measurement remains the single greatest challenge to social-media adoption by companies.
>
> While digital channels and online interactions offer a plethora of data points, they don't come with a set playbook

for assigning value. Marketers have grown comfortable with formulas like gross ratings points and frequency, time-tested formulas for building brands in traditional media. Yet with social media, what's a Facebook friend worth?[1]

Despite this lack of business-building metrics, marketers continue to spend money on social media:

> According to an ExactTarget survey of 1,000 marketers, 70 percent said they plan to increase spending in social media, but less than 20 percent said they could effectively measure ROI.[2]

Morgan Stewart, ExactTarget's director of strategy and research, believes that the leap of faith demonstrated by the numbers is "because marketers using social media tend to blend 'art and science' in their measurements." Stewart explains that "ROI isn't the thing that's pushing people to social media. . . . Companies using reputation as a measure of success are more likely to be shifting budget there. That tells you something about the mind-set."[3]

Twitter and Advertising—Using the Google Model

Twitter's acceptance of advertising tweets is one sign that it may understand the need for a measurable relationship to exist in order to impact the marketing and sale of a product or service. Will it be successful? According to *Advertising Age*, "Searches on trending topics are an inevitable place for mass market ads. But searches on other hashtags are also likely to generate interest from advertisers, and relevant ad tweets make sense here. If a T-shirt company puts ad tweets into searches on "Lady Gaga" and "#LadyGaga," good for them. As with Google, these ads will fit nicely into the organic searches."[4]

Does this mean that social networking is going back to the future—to advertising? Fox made a tremendous investment in that future when it bought MySpace. But technology users are fickle. Unless it has first-mover advantage, like Twitter—or is a game changer, like Google—people move on to the newest, coolest site that their friends are using. These days, Facebook is more popular (although facing significant criticism and negative feedback on its privacy policies) than MySpace, and Fox will probably find it has lost money on its investment.

However, the reality is that the vast majority of these sites make little if any money. They succeed or fail on buzz—that is what drives their valuation. So far, they simply don't have an effective economic business model for long-term success.

Reinventing the Relationship

Fox is a shining example of marrying buzz to a cultural zeitgeist while generating profits with its Fox News Channel. Roger Ailes, the head of Fox News and a former political consultant, has a remarkable ability to read the electorate and anticipate where it is headed.

Fox News was launched in 1996 during the second Clinton administration, a time when Americans and their representatives were polarized over a number of questions, including the direction of the country. Americans were passionate in their feelings about the Clintons, be they pro or con.

Fox News's main competitor is CNN, which prides itself on a nonpartisan approach to the news. In fact, at the urging of Jon Stewart, host of "The Daily Show with Jon Stewart" on the Comedy Channel, who during an appearance in 2004 criticized the program for "hurting America,"[5] CNN canceled its only program with a partisan outlook, "Crossfire."

While CNN programming throughout the day and night maintains its middle-of-the-road perspective, Fox in the evenings lets its hosts be themselves—which is, in many cases, conservative. Sean Hannity, Bill O'Reilly, and Glenn Beck lean to the right on most subjects. They are unafraid to stake out, and stand up for, positions that are in sync with the Republican Party. This is sometimes taken to the extreme: while promoting his memoir, *What Happened*, Scott McClellan, former White House press secretary (2003–2006) for former President George W. Bush, stated on the July 25, 2008, edition of "Hardball with Chris Matthews" that the Bush White House routinely gave talking points to Fox News commentators—but not journalists—in order to influence discourse and content.[6]

Fox News is genius at a number of things, but one of its greatest successes is in knowing its audience and building a relationship with them. Fox News decision makers know that, when it comes to marketing and ratings, everything old really is new again—it is all about continually reinforcing and reinventing the relationship.

And CNN? Well, according to the *New York Times*, CNN continued what has become a precipitous decline in ratings for its prime-time programs, with its main evening hosts losing almost half their viewers in a year. The trend in news ratings for the first six months of 2010 was all up for one network, the Fox News Channel, which enjoyed its best quarter ever in ratings, and down for both MSNBC and CNN.[7]

The ratings debacle led to the ouster of the head of CNN, Jonathan Klein, but at an interesting time—just after he had tinkered with CNN's prime-time schedule, replacing Larry King with Piers Morgan, best known for winning the first "Celebrity Apprentice" (Donald Trump's television show), and Campbell Brown's 8:00 P.M. (ET) show with one hosted by Kathleen Parker, a *Washington Post* columnist, and Eliot Spitzer, New York's disgraced former governor. On Klein's dismissal, the *New York Times* reported, "There has been a corporate bull's-eye on the back of Jonathan Klein, the president of CNN/U.S., for years, because of the stubbornly low ratings of his channel's prime time lineup. But it still came as a shock to many CNN employees when Mr. Klein was fired Friday, ending a six-year run at the head of the beleaguered cable news channel. After all, Mr. Klein had just set up a wholesale reinvention of CNN's prime-time schedule."[8]

Note to marketers: Reinvention does carry risk. But it also changes the game. The shining example of that remains Fox News, which created a paradigm shift for cable news.

In the beverage industry, Starbucks was also a game changer. Think about it—would anyone have paid five dollars for a cup of coffee 10 years ago?

Starbucks, founded in 1971, began as a small company known as much for its baristas' customer service as for its coffee. It built its reputation on delivering good taste to its customers while recreating the coffeehouse experience. In another era, soda shops served the same purpose—a place to get a drink while catching up with friends and neighbors. Say what you will about its expansion strategy, Starbucks customers are incredibly loyal. And that's not based on advertising—it's based on the relationship Starbucks has and continues to reinvent with its customers.

The Elements of the Relationship with the Consumer

Building a relationship with a consumer or customer is part of the science of marketing. In a world of 500-plus cable stations, Twitter, social networks, magazines, e-books, e-mail—simply hundreds (if not thousands) of media-based digital channels—garnering attention, let alone predisposition based upon exposure or direct interaction, is difficult.

Some brands do it by celebrity endorsement. Think of the impact that Michael Jordan and Air Jordans had for Nike. It not only differentiated the brand, it launched a new category. The Air Jordan is still the gold standard—none have ever had the impact of that one launch.

Others build their brand virally. Think of Red Bull, discussed in Principle #15. It took its brand directly to college students and built brand loyalty from there. And, once again, a category was created.

Still others go the traditional route—introducing a product or service brand positioning through advertising. That's what many larger companies still rely on to create awareness, favorability, and predisposition. For example, General Electric, which has multiple brands, continues to primarily use traditional broadcast and print advertising to support its "Imagination at Work" campaign, which underlies all of its products and services.

General Electric as a corporation truly lives its brand positioning statement: "GE is imagination at work. From jet engines to power generation, financial services to water processing, and medical imaging to media content, GE people worldwide are dedicated to turning imaginative ideas into leading products and services that help solve some of the world's toughest problems." All of its businesses are exhorted to "[harness] the power of the imagination to make life better for customers and consumers all around the world."[9]

Alternatively, I cannot think of one brand that has been launched through a social network that has captured the imagination of consumers. Yes, many brands have established "Friend" pages on Facebook. But what is increasingly apparent is that marketers recognize that social networks and sites like Twitter are secondary—not primary—marketing channels. When Twitter created an advertising-based revenue stream, it recognized its place. The question is, how many users will block these tweets?

As to the science of marketing, relationships with consumers and customers are built on knowledge and the application of insight and learning. Before launching any product or service, marketers should undertake extensive research to understand the product or service's targets, their preferences, their activities, their influencers—anything of applicable value that can be found out. These insights provide the foundation for marketing plans and ultimately for tactical campaigns.

Sustaining the Relationship

Marketing first creates the underpinning, which is the brand's brand positioning and marketing messages. Channels allow marketers to get these supporting messages out. All in all, use the process of building the marketing campaign and programs to build the relationship with the consumer or customer so that the product or service becomes something that is preferred and part of their routine—be it getting that Starbucks on the way to work or watching Bill O'Reilly in the evening to catch up with the events of the day and world.

One of the things airlines got right was loyalty programs. Earning mileage on an airline—to exchange for free tickets at a later date or for upgrades to business or first class—was a brilliant idea because it drove preference and repeat purchase. If a frequent flier lives in Atlanta, that flier is going to be singularly loyal (out of necessity) to Delta, since Atlanta is that airline's hub and earning Delta mileage is quick and relatively painless. It's the same in any hub city. People choose their airline (and hotels and car rental partners, as well as credit cards) based on acquiring mileage—sometimes choosing a more expensive carrier in order to earn the miles.

But loyalty programs also have their drawbacks, particularly when marketers use the data to push new products or try to take advantage of the relationship and don't value its sanctity. A consumer, Liz Miller, recalled her own experiences for an article on Brandweek.com:

> Just the other day I got an offer to get a credit card that would attach to my airline frequent-flyer card. . . . I got two e-mails about it, one from the credit-card company and another from the airline. Both told me about the fabulous offers and savings I could achieve, and even offered special bonuses if I joined. Then, I got three different mailings in my mailbox: one to Liz, one to Lisa and another to Elizabeth. Not sure who Lisa is, but she could get an even better offer than the one Liz received via e-mail. Here's the problem: I already have a card. In fact, I already got suckered for less savings, less reward, less bonus! So consumers are really learning that for every program or for every savings, you have to pay the piper, and you are going to pay with an avalanche of irrelevance that now could spread to your mobile phone.[10]

Simply put, there is no single digital channel that is the be-all and end-all for marketers. Marketers must understand that social networks are not the new marketing saviors. Carefully choose whether or not to participate, and do so expecting the return on investment may be low. Can social networks be used to create buzz? Absolutely, but it's a two-edged sword. Your company or enterprise cannot control the message.

REMEMBER

- Marketing equals relationship building.
- Marketing is based on knowledge and insights gained from research.
- Never launch a product or service until marketing knows all there is to know about your product or service's audience.
- And never ever take the relationship for granted. Treat it as you should and give it the value it deserves. Earn it every day.

You Don't Have to Go It Alone

Strategic partnerships can be brand-reinvention game changers, but they must be strategically undertaken.

Lewis and Clark. Romeo and Juliet. Ronald Reagan and Thomas P. (Tip) O'Neill. Tom Hanks and Meg Ryan. Booth and Bones. These partnerships succeeded because each half brought complementary abilities (and chemistry) to the table that took them from being merely good to memorable, if not great.

In marketing, partnerships are often used to reinvent a product or service to provide a halo effect to a brand. Partnerships can also be used to accomplish something that one brand alone cannot do without the assistance of another (assistance in the form of capital, contacts, core skills and competencies, or market permission, and so on).

For example, in 1999 Cisco Systems and the United Nations Development Program undertook a joint venture aimed at harnessing the power of the Internet to eradicate poverty globally. At that time, KPMG volunteered to partner with Cisco to develop the global website that would provide the capability for individuals around the world to watch three rock concerts that were happening simultaneously at Wembley Stadium in London, Giants Stadium in New Jersey, and the Palais des Nations in Geneva. NetAid originated the concept of real-time online charitable contributions and set the precedent for the groundbreaking types of Internet-based philanthropy later implemented during the aftermath of Hurricane Katrina and the earthquake in Haiti.

CNN and CBS seem to be in the process of creating a different type of partnership. In an era when network news budgets are constantly under pressure and news bureaus are closing around the world, CBS leverages the global reach of CNN as needed for reporting. In exchange, CNN anchors such as Anderson Cooper have the opportunity to host and be featured on high-profile shows on CBS such as "60 Minutes," which reaches many more viewers than any program on CNN.

From a marketing perspective, partnerships can be an effective means of achieving strategic objectives, ranging from overall brand recognition, enhanced brand reputation, general goodwill, and other important benefits.

As an example, during my tenure at KPMG, the firm's three strategic priorities were quality, people, and growth. To bring our focus on quality to life, we undertook the Global Initiative on Leadership and Business Ethics (the "Global Initiative") in partnership with the Norwegian Nobel Committee that awards the Nobel Peace Prize in Oslo each year.

The Global Center for Leadership and Business Ethics was the headquarters for the Global Initiative. It was founded on the conviction that leaders are defined by their actions and that those individuals who exhibit exemplary business ethics should be recognized and honored as a tangible way of recognizing and rewarding principled personal behavior and responsible business practices. This was very important at that point in time because auditors and business in general were held in low regard as the result of scandals involving Enron and WorldCom as well as other examples of corporate malfeasance.

The Global Initiative was a three-pronged effort that brought the "quality" imperative to life by creating the KPMG Global Center for Leadership and Business Ethics, the Laureate Award & Medal Series, and becoming the global founding partner of the Nobel Peace Center. The Global Center was founded on the premise that outstanding leaders do more than guide successful businesses or enterprises in producing economic returns to their stakeholders—they also serve as beacons of ethical personal behavior and responsible business practice. Through its Laureate

Award & Medal Series, the Center recognizes and promotes the attributes of accomplishment and innovation, stimulating the adoption of best practices in the marketplace.

This partnership with the Norwegian Nobel Committee was invaluable for KPMG. It was perceived by business and government leaders, regulators, and key constituencies as the penultimate representation of quality, one of its strategic objectives. It was of equal importance to Nobel, which was slowly and consciously entering the world of corporate sponsorships and was searching for additional platforms to extend its presence and relevance to other areas of global influence.

While the Global Center is an example of a private company–private organization partnership, there are also many examples of public (government)–private sector partnerships, especially as it relates to health and wellness globally, including the following:

» The Global Alliance for Vaccines and Immunization is financed 75 percent by the Bill and Melinda Gates Foundation, which has a permanent seat on its supervisory board.
» The TB Alliance, which partners with research institutes and private pharmaceutical companies to develop treatments for tuberculosis that are affordable and accessible to the developing world, is financed by public agencies and private foundations.
» The World Health Organization (WHO) is financed through the United Nations system by contributions from member states. In recent years, WHO's work has involved more collaboration with nongovernmental organizations and the pharmaceutical industry, as well as with foundations.

Marketing Sponsorships—All About Sports?

Marketers also undertake sponsorships—more often than not in sports—to reinvent their brands. The practice goes back a half century. According to Golf.com, "While athletes had done radio and television ads prior to 1960, it was McCormack's founding of IMG that year that was a moment that changed the game. When [the legendary golfer Arnold] Palmer became McCormack's first client—the deal was struck with a handshake—McCormack launched the idea of an athlete as a global brand."[1]

And the marriage of sports and marketing gained momentum. Today, marketing and sports are in many ways indistinguishable. The replacement for New York's Shea Stadium is Citi Field, named for Citigroup; the Houston Astros play at Minute Maid Park; the Carolina Panthers play at the Bank of America Center; NASCAR even has a sponsor, Sprint, for its championship series as well as for each of its races (for example, the Coca-Cola 600)—it just goes on and on, across all sports with the exceptions of some of the major Opens or Final games.

However, as often as marketers go to sports for a quick fix or easy solution, there are ways to reinvent sponsorships so they are not simply about sports. In almost all instances a marketer must be acutely aware of the potential for a skeptical reaction by the public. A company like Goldman Sachs (which we have criticized in certain portions of this book) can undertake a sponsorship—say, college scholarships, or raising money for homeless shelters, or funding an initiative such as 10,000 Women (a five-year investment through a network of more than 70 academic and nonprofit partners to provide 10,000 underserved women around the world with a business and management education)—to help to restore its tarnished reputation. By reaching out to the global or local community, its sponsorships and initiatives may over time change the way the firm is perceived—if it's not viewed cynically.

REMEMBER

- Look for a partner that shares your brand's business goals and objectives.
- Determine what type of partnership is appropriate for your brand and ensure it aligns with your reinvention strategy.
- Before you create a partnership stratagem, make sure you can expect a strong return on your investment. If you cannot justify a partnership or sponsorship on a ROI basis, decline the opportunity.
- Sponsorships, though most often identified with sports, are often a great way to build community relations and burnish a reputation.
- Sponsorships must be organic, or their impact can be lost to cynicism.

It's Not About You, It's Really About Me

Celebrity endorsements work, but they are a double-edged sword. As long as a company or enterprise is aware of the dangers and approaches endorsements cautiously, they can be successfully used for reinvention.

Often, marketers turn to a celebrity endorser in their efforts to reinvent their products or services, believing that there will be a halo effect. However, in an age of TMZ and tabloids, halos are easily tarnished, and celebrities more often than not can become a burden instead of a blessing.

Do these endorsements pay off for the company or enterprise that is leveraging the celebrity? Bob Greene, the award-winning columnist for the *Chicago Tribune*, writing at CNN.com, believes so, saying that when celebrities and athletes endorse a product, "not only is the public's disbelief suspended, but people don't seem to particularly care that the recommendation is bought and paid for."[1]

According to Greene, the bottom line supports this for marketers: "When celebrities are paid to say they like something, studies show, it generally translates into increased sales for the companies that hire them."[2]

Celebrity Endorsements and Marketing

The best and generally most effective endorsement deals equate the product or service with the celebrity. Perhaps one of the greatest partnerships of this kind in history is George Foreman and Salton, the maker of the George Foreman Grill. The George Foreman Lean Mean Fat Reducing Grilling Machine was first introduced in 1994 through late-night infomercials. George Foreman, the widely recognized and well-liked world heavy-weight boxing champion, fit both the "lean" and the "mean" aspects of the name, and he was a well-liked celebrity who connected easily with the public.

"Salton was looking for different spokespeople when the grill was first introduced," says Gary Ragan, vice president of marketing and product manager for Salton. "We needed a great product, but also a great personality that matched. George is like an everyman sort of guy. He's not telling you to go on this restrictive diet to eat healthy; he's just showing you how easy it is to do if you buy the grill."[3]

This partnership was so successful, in fact, that "In the end, the Foreman-fervor led to Salton's extremely expensive branding decision to buy the George Foreman name. Led by CEO Leonhard Dreimann in 1999, Salton signed Foreman to a five-year mega-deal worth $137.5 million (U.S.) for the worldwide rights to his name and likeness. The deal paid off for both parties; it sky-rocketed Salton to the top of the household product makers and allowed Foreman to branch off into his own business ventures."[4]

Celebrity Endorsements and the Fall from Grace

In terms of celebrity endorsements, the poster child for a fall from grace is undoubtedly Tiger Woods. For many years, Woods had a pristine, all-controlling, and somewhat distant image that many corporations—Accenture, Gatorade, Nike, General Motors, and American Express, to name a few—used to elevate their own brands. He was known as one of the world's most marketable athletes and was admired and respected by people of all ages.

Then came the fall from grace—a series of revelations about extramarital affairs, a sabbatical from golf that included an extended visit to a sex addiction clinic, a separation and later a divorce from his wife, and an odd news address in which Woods apologized, yet took time to berate the media for its constant coverage of his family.

During this period, many of Woods's sponsors left him, Accenture and Gatorade among them. Both companies felt that his image had or would further tarnish their brands. Accenture, specifically, had millions invested in Woods, in billboards all over the world. However, the global consulting firm believed that the damage to its corporate image—having its brand and Woods's visage associated in people's minds in almost every airport in the world—was worth the expense of unraveling, rebranding, and reinventing.

Conversely, although Nike's target is generally a young audience, many of whom felt Woods's fall from grace as a personal disappointment, Nike has stood by him—in fact, it created the first (and controversial) ad for him after his return to golf at the 2010 Masters. Why? Simple financial reasons: Woods's endorsement is a product approval for Nike—not only a brand endorsement—that "has been credited with playing a significant role in taking the Nike Golf brand from a 'start-up' golf company earlier in the past decade to the leading golf apparel company in the world and a major player in the equipment and golf ball market. Nike Golf is one of the fastest-growing brands in the sport, with an estimated $648 million in sales in 2009."[5]

So celebrity endorsements are definitely a double-edged sword. A *BusinessWeek* article made the following observation a few years back, one I agree with:

> The surest way to ensure long-term value from a celebrity spokesperson is to invent one. Advertising agency giant Leo Burnett pioneered this approach with Tony the Tiger, the Jolly Green Giant, and the Pillsbury Doughboy. Budweiser made hay with frogs and a lizard a few years back, and the roly-poly Michelin Man recently made a comeback (slimmed down for a more health-conscious culture).

Geico has done a masterful job making a little green gecko and big hairy cavemen famous. Since they're not real people, the risk of them doing something illegal, immoral, or embarrassing is nil, and the company can evolve their roles and storyline over time.[6]

For these reasons, before including a public figure in the marketing strategy, marketers must determine exactly what the celebrity's role will be and have the data-driven metrics to evaluate and continue its association for the long term, as Nike did.

Tiger's fall from grace impacted the business of celebrity endorsements. With that has come a change in the balance of power that existed between celebrities and the products and services that want to be affiliated with them. Now more than ever, companies are encouraged to take a more circumspect approach to attaching a brand to a celebrity, and to do a more complete background check. But in the end, it's still a game of chance.

As T. L. Stanley describes in *Brandweek*, many marketers should anticipate the possibility of an unexpected celebrity-driven event and plan accordingly:

Morals clauses—a staple of many contracts between individuals and entities, and a longtime stipulation in endorsement deals—are becoming more thorough and specific, as are the contracts the parties sign. These documents are more likely to lay out what constitutes a breach, as well as the penalties for a transgression. Since brands want to mitigate their risk, they often have a Plan B for their marketing should anything happen with their celebrity endorser.[7]

The Celebrity Endorser as "One of Us"

Jenny Craig, the weight management system, has used celebrity endorsements very strategically and effectively to continually reinvent its brand. Having long realized that its key audience is women who struggle with weight loss, they chose Kirstie Alley, who has had a very public battle with her weight, as one of their first spokespeople. For Ms. Alley, weight negatively impacts her ability to get roles as an actress.

Once the campaign began, Jenny Craig didn't just do "before and after" views of her success—it chronicled her battle in continuing ads and online in her blog. As the spokesperson, Ms. Alley was very open about the uphill battle she was facing. When she reached her goal weight and appeared on television and in *People* magazine in a bikini, others who faced the struggle at her age believed losing weight was possible for them, too.

However, the more important message communicated was that weight management is not easy, which became even clearer when Ms. Alley stepped down as celebrity spokesperson and out of the Jenny Craig maintenance program. Once off the program, she regained all her weight. While this is an unfortunate circumstance for Ms. Alley, it is a relatively strong (although backhanded) continuing endorsement of Jenny Craig and the necessity for long-term continuity and commitment to weight loss and maintenance. Ms. Alley is now on a weight-loss program that she has devised.

More recently, Valerie Bertinelli, someone most baby boomers remember from their television-watching youth (she played Barbara Cooper Royer on "One Day at a Time" and Gloria on "Touched by an Angel"), replaced Ms. Alley as celebrity endorser, and she has had a more straightforward, long-term success in the role. Again, Ms. Bertinelli appeals to Jenny Craig's target demographic, and she has been very open about her battle with her weight. She has remained as Jenny Craig's spokesperson as the company broadens its target audience to men. Now Ms. Bertinelli appears with "Seinfeld" star Jason Alexander, who reached his goal of losing 20 pounds before turning 50 using Jenny Craig, in addition to actress Sara Rue, who has to date lost 50 pounds on the program.

Jenny Craig's main competitor, Weight Watchers, has also recently moved to a celebrity endorsement model, using Academy Award–winning actress Jennifer Hudson as its spokesperson. One had not been associated with that brand in commercials since Sarah Ferguson did so at the turn of the century.[8]

In general, celebrity endorsements are very tricky and require contingency planning. They should be undertaken as part of a marketing plan only if the company is prepared to accept the bad that might come with the good.

REMEMBER

- Celebrity spokespeople are a double-edged sword when it comes to reinvention. Be prepared for both the good and the bad.
- Measure return on investment rigorously—in fact, incorporate metrics into the contract. It's the only way to know what a brand is getting from the association with a celebrity.
- Know your brand's audience and choose age-specific endorsers that speak to them—be they seniors, baby boomers, Gen X, or other targeted demographics.

The Long Arm of the Law

Regulation and new regulatory bodies directly impact reinvention efforts and the work marketing must do. A company can influence the issues, but it must never lose sight of the fact that a crisis, such as the recent Great Recession, can lead to new and unexpected regulations.

t seems just about every company or enterprise today, regardless of whether it is undertaking a reinvention-driven agenda, is regulated at some level by the government, its industry, or its peers. As a result, most marketers come to be intimately acquainted with their company's legal department. There are rules that govern how various industries may go to market, and if marketers (or for that matter CEOs) are not careful, they may unintentionally break them. That is why a marketer's best friends (and occasional adversaries) are oftentimes the lawyers in the office of general counsel.

The Landscape of Increasing Regulation

According to Ian Davis in the *McKinsey Quarterly*, the role of government regulation is increasing:

> Another defining feature of the new normal will be an expanded role for government. In the 1930s, during the Great Depression, the Roosevelt administration permanently redefined the role of government in the US financial system. All

signs point to an equally significant regulatory restructuring to come. Some will welcome this, on the grounds that modernization of the regulatory system was clearly overdue. Others will view the changes as unwanted political interference. Either way, the reality is that around the world governments will be calling the shots in sectors (such as debt insurance) that were once only lightly regulated. They will also be demanding new levels of transparency and disclosure for investment vehicles such as hedge funds and getting involved in decisions that were once the sole province of corporate boards, including executive compensation.[1]

In the past few years, the United States government has bailed out a number of industries, including the highly visible and controversial finance and automotive sectors. The Big Three automakers are an interesting case study in intervention.

In 1979, the government bailed out Chrysler—with little or no oversight. In 2009, during the Great Recession, Chrysler and General Motors were deemed "too big to fail," much like a number of financial institutions. Very simply, confidence in the U.S. economy would reach its nadir, it was believed, if any one of the Big Three went under during the Great Recession. So the federal government took $24.9 billion of the $700 billion bailout fund and made it available to the Big Three. Ford Motor Company turned down the bailout funds as previously discussed: it believed in its reinvention strategy and felt it was on the right track.

However, Chrysler, Chrysler Financial, GM, and GMAC (GM's financing arm) took the money—$17.4 billion for Chrysler and GM, $1.5 billion for Chrysler Financial, and $6 billion for GMAC. As a result, the government took an active interest in how this money was spent, naming a "car czar"—first Steven Rattner, then Ron Bloom—to lead the auto task force and help the companies restructure and reorganize.[2]

In the United States, whether a Democrat or a Republican is in charge, it seems that regulatory intervention ultimately mushrooms, regardless of the pendulum swing between deregulation and regulation. Big government seems to just get bigger each year. In the wake of the Great Recession, reforms in the financial industry were introduced and passed before the midterm elections in November 2010. Because of health-care reform, that industry will also undergo tremendous change. Both reform-driven industries will require marketers to reinvent their brands. And both industries will require reinvention in the face of these new regulations.

Reacting to Regulation—A Marketer's Case Study

With each of these reforms comes increased government scrutiny. My tenure at KPMG coincided with some of the biggest change in the history of the accounting industry. During that time, we saw the establishment of a new government oversight body—the Public Company Accounting Oversight Board, or PCAOB. Created in response to the systemic corporate failures at WorldCom and Enron, among others, the PCAOB does annual inspections of select audits an accounting firm performs. The goal of this type of intervention is to ensure that audits are performed independently and in line with a rigorous methodology.

In the context of my experience at KPMG, what does PCAOB oversight mean as it relates to marketing? Not only did it mean that the marketing teams worked closely with KPMG's legal and executive offices, it also provided a very real brand opportunity. KPMG chose a very specific and, at the time, highly controversial reinvention path in response to the PCAOB's closely watched first inspection report. Very simply, at a point in time when the Big Four were seen as being at best opaque in their transactions, KPMG chose to be completely transparent, underscoring the firm's "clarity" brand positioning.

For each issue identified by the PCAOB, KPMG provided the U.S. partnership's perspective, as well as the actions and steps KPMG had taken to address the issues and allay the regulator's concerns. Comprehensive and detailed response documents were created on how KPMG had improved the quality of the firm's audit methodology and risk management processes. The PCAOB findings were made available in two parts—Part I is made public, while Parts II and III are nonpublic. Therefore, KPMG also provided exhaustive responses to the Part II findings, which, though private, identified areas for improvement.

The marketing and communications task force then created a comprehensive set of materials, including the response, that was circulated to clients, prospects, employees, pending new hires, politicians, key influencers, and other regulators and interested parties, including the media. Marketing created these materials in both hard copy and electronic versions, so that as soon as the PCAOB made its limited inspection (in its first year the PCAOB had time to review only a limited number of audits) available publicly on its website, the firm could provide an immediate response to its thousands of clients and prospects—literally within minutes of the public release by the government.

Additionally, the firm provided its partners with talking points about the report to use with each and every client the next morning, as well as PowerPoint materials to use with boards of directors and audit committees. KPMG directly distributed its response to thousands of business leaders—and its answers were forthcoming and clear, thus reinforcing its strategic objectives and reinforcing the firm's brand positioning.

KPMG was the only firm to take the extra step of responding publicly to the PCAOB's findings. By so doing, it not only underscored its commitment to clarity, it set a standard for interactions by competitors with this new regulator as well as establishing a higher expectation of corporate America.

TARP and Regulation

In what seems a swing of the pendulum to a new age of never-ending regulation and government intervention, marketers can make a difference in building a relationship with the regulator. Marketers know the importance of being involved from the beginning in the development of a product or service. This form of involvement is easily transferred to working with grassroots and community organizations to make a company or enterprise's views known and impact regulations before they are written and sanctioned.

It is important to note that a company or enterprise should not enter any of these discussions with a regulator as an adversary. Rather, these types of exchanges and discussions on what's "wrong" with an industry and what needs to be fixed should be approached as in-market focus groups, with the company or enterprise's representatives listening more than speaking. Small changes early in the process can have a large impact in demonstrating an overall willingness to change without regulatory requirements or oversight.

A group of companies that in some instances don't (or at least don't appear to) listen are Wall Street's large financial institutions. Many of them received funds under the Troubled Asset Relief Program—TARP—which was funded solely by taxpayers. Originally put in place to help unfreeze the credit markets and because the U.S. Treasury found these institutions "too big to fail" (meaning their failure could take the U.S. and, perhaps, global economies down with them), TARP provided emergency money to just about every investment house on Wall Street, as well as to banks, in the hope that these institutions would then make this money available to businesses and homeowners and thus "unfreeze" the credit markets and also slow the foreclosure crisis.

TARP stabilized the financial institutions, but there was no apparent trickle-down effect—money was not freed up for investment in small businesses or for credit to help halt foreclosures. Instead, it seemed to the average American (whether true or not—perception is the real reality) that TARP money was used to reward executives with large bonuses—the same executives who had gotten the institutions into this mess in the first place, and who were held responsible by the public for increasing unemployment and home foreclosures.

At some point, you would think that these executives would understand the reaction to this news—the rising anger on Main Street, in Congress, and by the president. They did not. Instead, as Goldman Sachs executive Lloyd Blankfein infamously said, they continued to see themselves as doing "God's work," untouchable by the mere mortals who had bailed them out.

It is no surprise, then, that the response to this apparent arrogance was new financial regulations driven in part by politicians and political agendas, including a pay czar whose job it was to oversee pay and bonuses at companies that received TARP money. Such intervention seems to be the response of Washington to any crisis today—name a czar, a commission, or a new oversight body and then create new legislation.

To influence these bodies, marketers need to be invested from the beginning in groups that directly or indirectly impact the company or enterprise's industry. The company or enterprise needs to create relationships with congressional representatives in its districts as well as standing committee leaders and members, and with influential experts and association leaders in its industry. It needs to invest not only in lobbying, but also in research, to ensure that it is not like the Wall Street titans who went deaf at a critical and pivotal juncture in their history.

Is Anyone Listening?

Unfortunately, business doesn't seem to have learned the lesson. Recently, in the wake of the oil spill in the Gulf of Mexico, BP undertook a brand campaign to help its image with Americans. To date, that campaign has harmed the company more than helped it. When word leaked that the company had spent $50 million on such advertising (never confirmed by the company, but quoted by President Obama in a televised news conference on June 4, 2010, in Louisiana), residents of the Gulf and Americans in general were appalled. Starting a brand campaign in the middle of an environmental crisis was shortsighted if not just plain dumb—especially when people were complaining about a lack of responsiveness from BP on a variety of fronts, including meeting its obligation to making the fishermen and other workers in the Gulf whole by paying them for their losses.

And yes, there is a commission studying the BP oil spill. Expect new regulations for that industry, as well.

The reality is that clearly there is a political trend, if not a social trend, toward greater regulation, driven by the Great Recession, the oil spill in the Gulf, the global reach of financial institutions, and the complexity and interconnectivity of economies, among other macro factors. Leadership needs to ensure that going forward, marketing participates and collaborates to shape the environment in which companies and business enterprises exist.

Reputation, Regulation, and Reinvention

When trying to influence the environs and surroundings within which a business or enterprise exists, marketers and the companies or enterprises they work for must be keenly aware of their reputation above almost everything else, because it can determine whether or not their outreach is effective and taken seriously.

Once again, and by way of a continuing example, Goldman Sachs experienced this firsthand when company leaders were not invited to share their opinion of the new financial regulation by the Obama White House. According to the *New York Times*:

> Goldman Sachs employs perhaps the country's most well-connected stable of Washington lobbyists, and it spent $2.8 million last year to bend the ear of federal officials and lawmakers. But the pounding the investment firm has taken in recent days has left it sidelined—at least in public—as Congress moves toward a decision that could reshape the very industry it rules.[3]

Still, the company tried to find a way to influence the debate, even if it could not play a visible a role. One person briefed on its plans, but who spoke on condition of anonymity because of the firm's continuing legal and political troubles, said it was still trying to push its agenda. The financial reform package was passed and signed into law in the summer of 2010. Goldman's impact, if any, is unknown, although it did try to exert some influence through lobbyists and trade groups like the Securities Industry and Financial Markets Association and American Banking Association.

When Regulators Are Perceived as Failing: The BP Controversy

The Gulf oil spill began on April 20, 2010, when the Deepwater Horizon, an oil rig, exploded in the Gulf of Mexico off of Louisiana, killing 11 workers. That tragedy was just the beginning of an environmental disaster that will, many believe, contaminate the coasts of Louisiana, Mississippi, and Florida for decades.

On Monday, April 26—six days later—it became public knowledge that a leak had been discovered in the oil well the rig was working on. Original reports said there were only 1,000 gallons of oil a day leaking into the Gulf; later that number was raised to 5,000 gallons (making it a "spill") and, even later, to 11,000 to 19,000 gallons a day, making it the worst oil spill in history and an environmental disaster of unknown proportions. A number of attempts were made to stem the spill, but it continued until it was finally successfully capped and the relief well completed in September 2010.[4]

BP's regulator, the Minerals Management Service (MMS), an agency within the Department of the Interior, was seen as being as culpable in this disaster as BP, due to its cozy relationship with the companies under its watch and its lax oversight. The *Huffington Post* summarized the situation and the problems with the relationship between government and business as follows:

"Of greatest concern . . . is the environment in which these inspectors operate—particularly the ease with which they move between industry and government," wrote Acting Inspector General Mary Kendall. Kendall said the investigation found that even after starting job negotiations with Island Operating Co., an MMS inspector conducted four inspections of the same company's platforms—and found no problems. Soon after, the unidentified inspector resigned from MMS to work for the company.

The revolving door can undermine government regulation in several ways. Former government workers who move to industries they once regulated can take advantage of personal relationships at their former agencies on behalf of their new companies. They can exploit loopholes in regulations based on their knowledge of the federal bureaucracy. And even before leaving, government employees hoping to one day land high-paying jobs with companies they regulate might be tempted to ease off.[5]

And conflicts of interest and other poor decisions continued to plague the MMS office that was supposed to be regulating the oil industry. Shortly after the Deepwater Horizon tragedy, as oil was freely spilling into the Gulf, the *Washington Post* reported the following:

> An Interior Department inspector general's report details misconduct in the service's Lake Charles, La., office, charging that MMS inspectors routinely took gifts—including hunting trips, college football tickets and meals—from the companies they were supposed to be policing.[6]

To date, the agency has seen its director and a subordinate resign and/or be fired; other changes are sure to follow.

In this case, the regulators failed, and the company is accused of taking advantage of the regulators' weakness. There are no winners here. Undoubtedly, there will be tougher regulation, but the loss of confidence in government and in BP and, in turn, Big Oil cannot be quickly regained. Here reinvention must be applied to a government agency (as well as BP)—it must go back to the reason it was created and rebuild itself.

REMEMBER

- Listen and learn: use research to understand emerging trends in your brand's industry, listen to customer and consumer reaction to them, and learn how to address the root issues consumers or customers may have with the industry.
- Participate early in crafting legislation and in becoming a member of emerging-issues task forces to shape the environment your business exists in.
- Use lobbyists to influence the situation and government officials.
- Work with influential experts and regulators to create a setting that is flexible enough to change, yet stable and robust enough for a company or enterprise's success.

INFRASTRUCTURE IS MORE THAN JUST PIPES

MORE OFTEN than not, the actual alignment of marketing with a company or enterprise's P&L and the parallel organizational design of marketing (and, for that matter, communications) are given short shrift. It's often a secondary consideration that is not given its full due because of legacy, operating, or internal political considerations. Surprisingly little thought is given to the role of marketing and its impact on driving profitable revenue and market share growth.

Oftentimes, technology and business analytic tools that can serve as the foundation for implementing a reinvention strategy are equally shortchanged. These valuable tools, when coupled with a robust knowledge management system, can dramatically impact a reinvention agenda and the creation of real value from a company or enterprise's intellectual and knowledge-based assets and the resulting competitive intelligence stratagem.

There's a Reason
It's Called the Center

Within a marketing organization, there is always tension
between national headquarters and the field. However,
creating a marketing organization that is managed and
run from the center is key to developing an integrated
team that understands not only the reinvention strategy,
but also the context in which it was created.

T he organization that puts reinvention theory into action is
marketing. Marketers are the conduit, the key ambassadors, and the epicenter of expertise. Where the marketing
team takes direction, how it is organized, and its role could spell
success or failure for a company or enterprise's strategic and revenue imperatives.

As long as I have been a marketing professional, there has
been a debate about where the power should lie—with the central or national headquarters or localized in the field. There is
usually a great deal of tension between the marketers on the
ground—nearest the buyer—and those at the national level, with
neither side believing the other understands (or knows how to
exploit) what is really happening in the marketplace.

At KPMG, the partnership has experienced both organizational models. When I first joined the firm, the P&L lines ran
through the geographic areas, or field, so marketing was controlled at the local level. Marketing budgets were dispersed and
spent locally. No one knew what was being spent on marketing

because marketing funds were held in so many buckets under so many titles by so many people. That is not the optimal way to allocate—let alone effectively spend (and measure)—marketing dollars.

When I joined the firm as its first and only externally hired chief marketing officer, I was tasked with centralizing marketing and using the field primarily for implementation and feedback. This was not an easy undertaking—the 1,800-plus partners did not want to lose "their" marketing people, nor did they want to lose the financial resources associated with those individuals. Partners felt they knew best how to serve their clients and their locality, as well as their area.

What these area and local office partners lacked, more often than not, was a broad view of strategy, firm priorities, and where the firm wanted to go. As a result, the area's marketing person was not linked to any particular national strategy, and in some cases this person was used by the partner as a glorified adminis-trative assistant. There was little or no contact with the national headquarters, which was viewed by many as "back office" or a place to get brochures produced.

Reorganizing Is Never Easy

The first surprisingly difficult task was simply to identify the marketing and communications professionals in the local offices, areas, functions, and industries. To do so, one of the existing area directors—known and respected by the market-ers in the field—was assigned with meeting one-on-one with the area partners and each local office managing partner, as well as with the marketers, to determine what was actually going on in the field. She was also asked to evaluate the talent so we could determine what gaps existed and decide what needs were going unmet. We then created a standardized organization chart show-ing roles and responsibilities for each area, with communicators and marketing personnel reporting in to the national office. This seemingly easy assignment took almost two years to uncover all the human capital resources hidden in a largely dispersed organization of 22,000-plus.

Concurrently, we created separate but similarly structured marketing and communications organizations that served the audit, tax, and advisory functions. At this point, the operating P&Ls had transitioned to these functions from the geographic areas. Therefore, these area-based marketing and communications teams were the largest within the overall marketing and communications organization, which totaled more than 550 professionals. The teams were also supported by an industry team focused on the 18 sectors or industry segments in which KPMG had unique and specialized capabilities and services. In this matrixed organization, while we clarified reporting lines, it was imperative that the marketing and communications professionals work across them to accomplish the firmwide vision and national objectives.

To optimize productivity and brand management, we also created national shared services groups comprised of creative services (copywriters, art directors, designers, editorial oversight, proofreading, and production services), research, proposal strategy and development, Web design and technology, brand and regulatory compliance, and brand management. These centralized shared service teams' key clients were the other functional and industry marketing groups, as well as the area-based teams and, importantly, the firm's leadership at the executive office.

Communications was split into corporate and internal teams. Each of these teams had people at both the national and area level, with alumni communications responsible for ongoing interaction with former KPMG partners and employees also located in the field.

The change brought about by the reinvention of marketing was not easy for the partners or the organization, but it was necessary, simply because it got marketing and communications people a seat at the table, and it produced results. Our key internal clients were KPMG's leadership team (of which I was a management committee member), which developed the firm's strategy. Most of the leadership team members were located in New York, and all major meetings were held in New York (with the exception of the annual partners' meeting, which was held in Orlando).

A Seat at the Table

Why is a seat at the leadership table so important for a marketer? To do the job as well as marketers are expected to, it is simply not enough to know the strategy. Marketers must understand how the company or enterprise reached its strategy—what key drivers set the company on this path and why this strategy is seen as both achievable and aspirational. Without that context, it is difficult, if not impossible, to craft a well-reasoned reinvention strategy that encompasses, addresses, and resolves the issues of concern of leadership.

For this reason I believe that it is imperative for a company or enterprise to be nationally driven (or globally if the company or enterprise is worldwide). A brand is diffused and loses its credibility if it has 2,000 different positionings (the number of partners in KPMG who might be asked to describe the firm). A centrally based team that controls and uses frameworks flexible enough to be customized at the local level but embedded in the national or global strategy ensures consistency in brand positioning, messaging, and management.

This national or global model works for the clothing store Zara, as profiled by the *McKinsey Quarterly*:

> Over the past few years, the Spanish retailer Zara, which overtook Gap in 2008 as the world's largest clothing retailer, has been a poster child for supply chain excellence because of its ability to deliver new items to stores quickly. . . . To ensure that the data are widely shared, Zara locates designers, marketing managers, and buyers in the company's La Coruña headquarters, where they work in open-plan offices. Frequent discussions, serendipitous encounters, and visual inspection

help teams diagnose the overall market situation, see how their work fits into the big picture, and spot opportunities that might otherwise fall between the cracks of organizational silos.[1]

Centralizing a Global Organization

The larger question becomes, how is a global company managed from the center? The utilization of frameworks is the key, as is flexibility for local or field operations to customize the frameworks. The *McKinsey Quarterly* posits the following for what the authors call "multilocal" organizations:

To get the balance right in a multilocal organization, companies should:

>> Find the value. To start, managers must understand, subfunction by subfunction, the size and nature of the cross-border and local value at stake. The greater the cross-border value, the more appropriate a relatively centralized model is likely to be.

>> Understand the barriers. In addition to identifying a company's potential sources of cross-border value, executives must identify the organizational barriers to achieving it. Our experience and research in Europe's power, banking, and telecom sectors have helped us identify three such barriers: a lack of awareness, poor motivation, and an inability to execute.

>> Consider the full range of organizing options. Some managers of multilocals, seeing only a choice between outright centralization and complete local independence, take an unrealistically narrow view of the way companies can organize functions. In reality, the choices and designs should be more nuanced.[2]

REMEMBER

- Managing marketing from the center and using frameworks locally makes achieving consistency simpler, creates monetary savings, and is more effective.
- For marketers to have a seat at the table and contribute effectively to a company's goals, they need to be located where leadership is located—usually at headquarters—and all leaders must have a clear and definitive understanding of the role of marketing.
- Local marketing organizations are invaluable in feeding back trends and in providing insight on the marketplace.

Technology Is Only the Enabler

Marketers are often distracted by the latest technology— companies want to be "on it" because it's there, not always necessarily because it's an appropriate and effective channel. Technology enables reinvention, not the other way around.

n 2009 and 2010, the news media was atwitter about Twitter. In 2009, it was because that social network was used to get news out of Iran, which had closed itself to reporters in the wake of a divided election. Many Iranians took to the streets to protest the election results because they did not believe that Mahmoud Ahmadinejad had won fairly. They made their support for the man they believed was the rightful leader, Mir-Hossein Mousavi, known—and suffered at the hands of Iranian security forces for it.

The world at large found out many details about the protest through Twitter, where photos and videos of security forces turning on civilians were posted. One video in particular first made available on Twitter—that of a young woman named Neda peacefully protesting and being shot dead by soldiers— brought the life-or-death reality of the marches home to people across the globe. In fact, the "Neda video," as it is known, was the first anonymous video to win the Polk Award, one of the most prestigious prizes in U.S. journalism, in February 2010.[1]

Twitter was also one of the first outlets to bring information and video on the earthquakes in Haiti and Chile. As a result of its wide reach, the Library of Congress archives all public Twitter updates.[2]

Some other interesting Twitter tidbits (as of April 2010):

>> It has more than 105 million registered users. Three-fourths of its online traffic comes from outside Twitter .com, through third-party services like TweetDeck and DestroyTwitter.

>> It posts 55 million tweets a day and serves 600 million searches daily.[3]

Twitter is not a news site, though—it is more correctly called a microblogging site, since users are limited to 140 characters per "tweet." Primarily a social networking site, Twitter is most often about the mundane experience of daily life. It is where people turn to talk about "American Idol" or "Dancing with the Stars" results, tell followers what they had for breakfast, and share information on their favorite music.

Twitter is also not, or at least hasn't yet proven to be, the be-all and end-all in marketing and reinvention. Much like the dog in the Disney-Pixar's movie *Up* was distracted by squirrels, marketers often find themselves overly engaged and engrossed by the latest technology. Unfortunately, marketers sometimes see technology as the reinvention end-all. It is not. It is only an enabler.

What these technologies are superb at marketing is themselves. In fact, Twitter, Facebook, MySpace, and other social media, like all marketing tools or channels, are simply the beginning—one tool or channel in an entire arsenal of reinvention tools and digital channels.

Technology's Impact on Marketing

Technology should, however, change the way that marketers approach marketing. In fact, many books have been written about the marketing revolution inspired by various applications and technology platforms. But marketers generally don't adapt to technology very well; rather, they try to adapt the old ways of doing things to the new technology. They redecorate rather than reinvent. Needless to say, marketers also generally fail in these excursions into new technologies.

At the end of the day, Facebook and Twitter and others of their ilk are simply communications tools or digital channels. On Facebook, a consumer can become a "fan" of a product or service, and if it gets enough followers, marketers can undertake some research, but what cannot happen is the marketing of a product or service to a new audience. The application proscribes this use. Only those who run Facebook can go to all its users with announcements. A brand manager cannot target all Facebook users or all Twitter users—only those in the product or service's network can receive information from an account. What consumers use these social networks for is to create their own communities—ones that can be made impenetrable to marketers.

Not being on Facebook or Twitter, however, can be seen as a marketing failure by corporate executives. How best, then, to use these digital channels for reinvention? Stores like Sephora use Twitter to tell "insiders" about special deals or to give a preview of sales. *Lucky* magazine uses Twitter to offer its readers discounts and advice, as do other magazines. But no product or service seems to have broken the code on how to market on Twitter—the code being the all-important driving of profitable sales and incremental revenues.

This is not a new trend, just a more difficult one given the quickly changing Internet-driven world. An article in *BusinessWeek* puts it this way:

> Corporate bean counters, who have long deemed marketing a squishy discipline, increasingly are demanding data to prove that a CMO's strategy is valid. One of the first things Cammie Dunaway did upon taking the CMO job at Yahoo! in 2003 was to hire a consultant to track return-on-investment for her marketing department. But Dunaway, who left to take the top sales and marketing job at Nintendo last October, says: "Your peers are always suspicious you have ordered up your own proof of

accountability." Her next move was to enlist Yahoo's own CFO to handle the analysis. "When you have the CFO's staff making marketing's case, instead of trying to make your case to the CFO," she says, "the credibility spreads fast."[4]

Technology Is Just Another Channel

As stated previously, instead of looking for the "savior" for their marketing efforts, marketers must understand that technology is only an enabler. New technologies enable marketers to get marketing messages out to a specific audience. Once again, however, technology is a double-edged sword—social media are also places where consumers and customers go to vent and complain about products or services, and good marketers must have a response mechanism in place when that occurs.

Therefore, marketers must treat digital technology like they treat every other channel. And the first question marketers must ask is what is the return on investment (ROI)? Is it worthwhile to spend time and/or money creating a presence here—let alone a for-profit business model?

Take newspapers, for example. Newspapers are in real danger of becoming dinosaurs thanks to digital technology. No newspaper has broken the code on how to leverage digital technology to make up for dwindling advertising and subscriber revenues. Yet some continue to make their content available, free. The *New York Times*, for example, has a robust application available for the iPhone—free. It is updated continually throughout the day. CNN and the *Washington Post*, however, charge for their iPhone applications, or "apps."

Subscribers can also get the *New York Times* breaking news alerts, free, on Twitter, as well as on Google News. And where once the *Times* had a paywall that required users to pay for a subscription to use its online services, it has since taken it down, though the company's leaders are reportedly thinking about reestablishing it for certain sections, such as Opinion. Why would anyone pay for a hard copy of the *Times*, given its widespread availability at no cost? And why would the leaders of the *Times* think that subscribers would pay for some content, after years of getting it free? The *Times* is suffering from lack of a clear marketing and content-driven digital technology strategy.

One has to wonder how the *New York Times* would be doing financially if it had charged for its content from the very beginning like the *Wall Street Journal* and the *Financial Times* did. Instead of seeing the Internet and the various technology applications as new digital channels for information and approaching them strategically, the *Times* rushed to be on them. The company has been making up for that apparent lack of a reinvention strategy ever since—as has the almost the entire newspaper industry. (*Newsday*, in an effort to induce trial customers, has turned its paywall into a premium giveaway for Cablevision subscribers.) Unfortunately, the news continues to be discouraging for the printed word. In late December 2010, eMarketer reported that online advertising in the U.S. will exceed newspaper advertising for the first time ever, with online advertising spending increasing by 13.9 percent to $25.7 billion. Conversely, newspaper ads declined 8.2 percent to $22.8 billion during the same time period.[5]

The lesson learned here is one discussed earlier: approach all reinvention with a strategy. Do not assume that because "everyone" is on Facebook or Twitter a certain product or service should be there as well. Do the necessary research and find out if members of the brand's target audience are regular users of a particular digital technology and if being on it creates preference and ultimately leads to profitable sales and increased revenues. If these platforms and applications are simply ways of interacting socially, does it really make sense for the company or enterprise to spend precious marketing dollars on these channels? Probably not.

One digital technology that may make sense for newspaper publishers, including the *New York Times*, is to offer newspaper subscriptions on Apple's iPad or similar platforms. The *Wall Street Journal* reported that Apple has had conversations with a variety of magazine and newspaper publishers, including Time Warner, Condé Nast, News Corp., and Hearst. As of this writing, the status of each organization is still unclear, as the *Journal* describes:

> It isn't clear whether publishers are jumping on board, but Apple has told them there is at least one company willing to sell its subscriptions through an Apple storefront, said a person familiar with the matter. Hearst has been more accommodating to Apple's subscription offering than some of the other large publishers, according to people familiar with Hearst's thinking.
>
> Some publishers say the ability to peddle their wares to the 160 million Apple account holders outweigh any loss of control in working with Apple.[6]

Reputation Management and Twitter

All marketers should monitor these new or emerging technologies and applications to see what is being said about their companies or enterprises. Although these digital channels are not always effective tools for marketing a product or service, the social channels—particularly Twitter—are a place where consumers and customers go to vocally voice their opinions and complain. And when they receive no response, their friends also complain. Customer service leaders must also be aware of the perception of their brand on Twitter and must swiftly move to counter or respond to any complaints.

Take, for example the case of Howard Kurtz and Dell. An influential reporter who covers the media for the *Washington Post* and also hosts a television show about the media on CNN, Kurtz is an inveterate Twitterer with more than 20,000 followers. His Dell computer crashed after only one year, and given a warranty that he paid extra for, he thought he would be fine. Instead, after repair technicians from Dell had been there, the computer still didn't work, and he joined the chorus of people trending on the topic "#dellfail" on Twitter. (Not a place any product or service wishes to be.) It is the marketer's (or communicator's) job to monitor the consumer or customer response—and respond quickly and positively before irreversible damage is done.

According to the sales and marketing trade publication *MarkeTech*:

There are three key metrics involved in what is referred to as "Online Reputation Management":

1. Share of Voice. This is a measurement of how much and to what degree people are talking about you.
2. Tone of Voice, a.k.a. "Sentiment analysis." This is a measurement of whether the conversation is largely positive or negative. If the sentiment is positive, reward those who speak well of you. If the tone is largely negative, you need to take action to get to the root of the problem IF one really exists. If it's based in misinformation, you'll need to engage the critics and correct their misunderstanding.
3. Trends over Time. It's important to monitor the above metrics over time to see the effects of your advertising, marketing and public relations efforts.[7]

The idea of viewing technology strategically may be new to most marketers. Most marketers tend to react: if their competition is there, the majority of marketers believe they must be there, too, no matter whether it fits (and actually benefits) their reinvention plans or not. And while plans must be flexible, if they are built strategically, with the core essence of the product or service in mind, then marketers should know whether technology fits into their strategy. And, the impact to the bottom line must be measurable.

Never lose sight of the fact that marketing exists to drive profitable sales and increased revenue. If an application or technology isn't going to accomplish those objectives, as a marketer you must question its suitability for the product or service—and appropriateness to your allocation of marketing expenditures and budget.

Also remember that technology changes at warp speed, as do consumer preferences for said technology—today's Kindle lover is tomorrow's iPad-only user. Do not become wedded to any one technology or platform as a means or method of marketing. Consumers and customers are as entranced by technology as marketers are. There is no longer such a thing as "early adopters"—everyone wants to try the newest, latest technology because users are looking for the holy grail—the technology that *will* save them time, not make them more frantic. Therefore, it may pay to be informed and aware of technology, but to save marketing resources for digital channels that have an actual, measurable payoff. In fact, marketers may need to not only review but also reinvent their relationship with technology in creating marketing plans.

The Future of Retail?

Online sales are an increasingly important digital channel for retailers as they reinvent this industry sector of our economy. Most if not all stores are online today, and the future of retail seems, with each passing month, more and more to be on the Internet. This would mean a true and fundamental change in the nature of the industry. As the first online-only retailer, Amazon is an example of what the future may ultimately hold—no salespeople, only customer service representatives.

With online sales topping \$156 billion in 2009,[8] a rise of 11 percent, it is no surprise that technology is such a focus for retailers. Indeed, much of the rise in online sales is coming at the expense of physical or "brick and mortar" stores. However, most retailers by now have made the strategic decision to make their merchandise available online. Some, such as Nordstrom's, allow customers to order online and pick up in-store, hopefully driving traffic to their physical buildings. The long-term success of this reinvention strategy is still up for discussion and appears to vary from retailer to retailer.

Nordstrom's and Saks are interesting in that both stores own lower-price brands where they sell out-of-season merchandise—Nordstrom Rack and Saks Fifth Avenue Off 5th. Neither of these reduced-price brands is online. So, at least for these two venerable clothing retailers, customers still need to head to brick and mortar stores for end-of-season bargains, despite the availability of these retailers' well-trafficked online sites. However, both companies send e-mail updates to customers to raise awareness of happenings and special events at these stores, and Nordstrom acquired HauteLook, the private sale website that popularized the online sample-sale format, for $180 million in February, 2011.

In the end, however, the necessity for the reinvention of the retail business model is a given. Technology will drive marketers to move their interactions with consumers ever closer to the actual point of sale via targeted promotional offers and the combination of smart mobile-equipped in-store buyers using price comparison apps such as TheFind or Amazon's Price Check, which will force ever greater price transparency. For those retailers without a corresponding strategy, the result will be a loss of sales revenues and ever greater profit erosion.

REMEMBER

- Approach applications, platforms, and new technology as you do any other channel.
- Determine the strategic value technology brings to your product or service, which digital channels to leverage, how often, and aimed at what audience.
- Be aware of what is being said about your product or service online— and be prepared to deal with the noise and chatter immediately.
- Technology is as much about communications as it is about marketing, and it has the ability to reshape industries (such as retail) quickly and for the long term.

Right Information, Right People, Right Time, Wrong Thought

Thought leadership can be the prized outcome of a
reinvention strategy. It's the upshot and outcome of
intense and nonpolitical internal collaborative processes
built on the foundation of reinvention frameworks created
by brand managers and marketing directors.

O ne of the most misunderstood and underappreciated (as well as minefield-laden and, at times, all-out political) processes within many companies is knowledge management, "the process through which organizations generate value from their intellectual and knowledge-based assets."[1]

In today's Internet-oriented world, the promise of knowledge management is big, and the payoff even larger if successfully implemented as a part of a reinvention initiative—but the downside is staggering financially when implementation is an abject failure and its goals go unrealized.

The reason? At risk are the millions of dollars of investment capital in not only hardware and proprietary software development but also in human capital resources that in a large international company must be deployed (both initially and over the long term) across national boundaries, cultures, and various diverse groups such as operations, sales, marketing, finance, and information technology to gather "knowledge content."

The codification of "what employees, partners and customers know, and sharing that information among employees, departments and even with other companies in an effort to devise best practices"[2] can be daunting and all consuming, but the result can be thought leadership.

Is thought leadership always the outcome of learning how to manage knowledge? For the marketer, it must be, and that is why knowledge management must be reinvented.

Knowledge Management Failure: A Case Study

When I was at KPMG, we sought to create a knowledge management team. As a firm, KPMG has the attributes of a global member organization for which knowledge management is essential. While it is a business built on shared methodologies—for an audit, or for understanding and applying complex tax regulations, for example—the distinction and potential differentiator is how its people effectively and efficiently apply the wisdom and knowledge they have gained over years of working for clients. (And I do mean wisdom—the application of skills and insights—not merely proficiency.)

Transferring that knowledge in a worldwide organization of member firms totaling 120,000-plus employees with an accepted industry standard of approximately 20 percent turnover annually was a challenge—one that the international chief executive officer handed to a technology executive to coordinate globally. Having incubated a dedicated knowledge sharing team for two years in marketing and communications at the national level, I knew the challenges the executive would face—specifically, gathering knowledge in a culture that was, for the most part, focused solely on delivering services to clients without stopping to think about transferring and sharing how that work was done. It just was—normally done incredibly well.

Within marketing and communications, we spoke the language that the audit, tax, and advisory professionals did because we worked side by side with them every day. As a result, we approached knowledge management as a means of sharing best practices and creating case studies in how the firm excelled—very simply, as a means of positioning our professionals and leaders, whom we felt differentiated us in the marketplace as thought leaders. And we found people interested in sharing that story, if they could understand how it would be used.

Ultimately, the then-chairman made the decision to move knowledge management to technology for what the leadership team viewed as a valid reason: knowledge management was seen as content gathering, and that was perceived by most senior managers as driven by technological processes.

Few within the firm saw technology as an enabler to anything because, honestly, the organization at that time was behind the curve in automating its processes, and because IT itself was a bureaucratic behemoth. Assigning knowledge management to technology was viewed as a way of bringing KPMG's technological processes into alignment with and surpassing those of our competitors, and as a way of catapulting technology to the forefront of the organization's thinking. And the leaders planned to accomplish all of those visionary goals through a $100 million content management system called KWorld.

So, the strategic imperative behind knowledge management was not to accumulate wisdom; rather it was about enhancing the firm's technological capabilities and processes. As such, it was bound to fail from the get-go.

The KPMG knowledge management team chose to define knowledge management for the firm as a way of collaborating, and it focused its efforts on creating joint collaboration spaces for teams and clients (KWorld). The project partially succeeded, but it failed in collecting the firm's acquired wisdom. The team also was unable to create a firmwide content management system—one of its primary objectives—because, in a budget-driven move, the responsibility for content gathering, conversion, and production was shifted to the service lines (audit, tax, and advisory) of the business without corresponding budgets for dedicated human capital resources and content managers. Unfortunately, politics and budgets got in the way of implementation, and the multimillion-dollar effort was destined, as a result, for a less-than-stellar outcome.

Under the Radar: Creating Thought Leadership

Notwithstanding this failure, managing and sharing wisdom was successfully accomplished in marketing and communications, where we created what later became three different teams—two teams that ended up being "institutes" focused on thought leadership for audit committees and on audit quality, and an internal team, the "Insiders," that daily created and shared select industry-oriented thought leadership. This group, which had many former journalists as members, created daily industry updates from the day's news, mixed with proprietary analysis and insights for thousands of current and prospective clients.

We were able to accomplish this feat because analysis, data mining, and understanding customers were rightly viewed as marketing's role, and marketing was rightly seen as being best suited to turn information into knowledge that would be valuable to clients and prospects. The by-product of this "information transformation" was thought leadership.

The Elements of Knowledge Management

Among the reasons that knowledge management was an ongoing struggle at KPMG was that the firm didn't fully understand the elements of knowledge management. Paul Brown details the key pieces in the *New York Times*:

> Typically a knowledge management process involves: knowledge capture; knowledge organizing and knowledge storage; knowledge distribution; knowledge sharing. . . . Successful knowledge management results in the best possible means to apply and leverage the knowledge that has been captured, organized and stored, distributed and shared. It means that very little of the company's highly valued intellectual capital has escaped the knowledge management net. Virtually all the knowledge within the enterprise is harnessed, and will be used as part of the company's core business and competitive intelligence strategy.[3]

CIO.com also presents a perspective on effective knowledge management, stating that it should help a company do at least one of the following:

» Foster innovation by encouraging the free flow of ideas
» Improve customer service by streamlining response time
» Boost revenues by getting products and services to market faster
» Enhance employee retention rates by recognizing the value of employees' knowledge and rewarding them for it
» Streamline operations and reduce costs by eliminating redundant or unnecessary processes[4]

Each of the goals that CIO.com lists is exactly what a reinvented marketing organization should do. Knowledge management is analogous to data mining—with employees as the customers, their wisdom as their preference, and the journey to quantify and qualify their wisdom and turn it into a product the role of product or brand managers.

Turning Knowledge into Thought Leadership

Very simply, knowledge is a core asset of a company or enterprise. The capture, transfer, distribution, and promotion of this knowledge in the form of thought leadership affects and influences not only internal human capital resources, but also the predisposition of both customers and prospects.

In early 2010, Gartner, a global leader in research and technology, announced the following:

While thought leadership has been used by consulting firms for a long time—often accounting for as much as 20 percent of marketing expenditure—an organized discipline of TLM (thought leadership marketing) is only now emerging, allowing marketers to use this as a manageable tool to drive business.

Gartner defines TLM as the giving—for free or at a nominal charge—of information or advice that a client will value so as to create awareness of the outcome that a company's product or service can deliver, in order to position and differentiate that offering and stimulate demand for it. Gartner's review of the TLM activities of IT services providers has shown three types of programs. These are not mutually exclusive but will often be combined:

>> Opportunistic. This type of program tends to be short-term and promotional-campaign focused. It boosts interest in and therefore sales of a specific offering.
>> Door-opening. This type of program can help establish or expand permission to play and is ongoing, although it evolves as acceptance grows to build visibility and credibility in the market.
>> Brand support. This is the most sustained type of TLM program and is used to reinforce the brand promise and image.[5]

Reinforcing the brand promise and image is exactly what thought leadership is all about—and for marketing, it can be a powerful tool to raise awareness of, interest in, and predisposition for a service or product. Thought leadership demonstrates competency and value creation; knowledge management claims competency.

Thought Leadership in Action: McKinsey & Co.

McKinsey & Company is considered by many the best at thought leadership creation, distribution, and promotion. An overview of the book *The McKinsey Way* gives an outline of the company's evolution:

In the early 1970s, the firm felt that, after 50 years, its growth was slowing. An internal committee reported that the firm had been neglecting the development of its professional and technical skills and was losing ground to new competitors that emphasized "thought leadership" rather than local client relationships.

McKinsey set up working groups to develop knowledge in two key areas: strategy and organization. . . . But still, most internally developed knowledge remained undocumented, because of a suspicion held by many consultants about trying to package ideas.

In 1987, McKinsey launched a knowledge-management project, which recommended that the firm build a common database of knowledge accumulated from client work. It also recommended that each practice area hire a person to act as an "intelligent switch" to monitor the quality of the data and help consultants find the information they needed.

From this project came three important tools:

>> A computer database of client projects (the firm's practice information system)
>> An initial database of 2000 documents prepared by each practice group, representing their core knowledge (the practice development network)
>> A list of specialists and key document titles (the knowledge resource directory)[6]

And McKinsey's efforts in thought leadership paid off, taking 9 percent of the market. Its closest competitor (PA Consulting Group) had only 5 percent.[7]

As a strategic consulting firm, thought leadership is a key element of McKinsey's brand persona. It markets ideas and strategies that promise to deliver profitable growth for businesses—and that is nowhere better evidenced than on https://www.mckinseyquarterly.com, its online site for the *McKinsey Quarterly*, where the company's accumulated wisdom is housed. It is one of the few online sites where an individual can gain access to the firm's work simply by registering, and it is a powerful marketing tool in itself.

The Future of Thought Leadership

The advent of Internet-based technology has given anyone with an opinion the ability to make himself or herself a self-styled thought leader. But, again, that is claimed competency. Marketing must use the knowledge that is accumulated within a company or enterprise to demonstrate competency. That demonstrated competency can serve as part of the foundation for the core essence of a product or service.

REMEMBER

- Reinvention means reexamining how we use the accumulated wisdom of our people. That wisdom may include an understanding of the customer that has not factored into our product or service development plans.
- Marketers know how to use demonstrated competency with consumers. Oftentimes, people don't know what they know—and marketers are uniquely positioned between the company or enterprise and its customers or prospects to glean and analyze information and turn it into thought leadership—something of real value.
- Knowledge management is as much about the customer as it is about the employee. Understanding the customer is essential to reinventing marketing.

RULE SIX
LEAD AND OTHERS WILL FOLLOW

N THE summer of 2010, a mine collapse trapped 33 miners underground in Chile. This tragic event captivated people around the world, and the miners' successful rescue was followed live by millions of fascinated viewers everywhere. Ultimately, after more than two months, every trapped miner was saved, and they became national heroes.

That's not how it began, however. At first, there was disorder and fear. Then their supervisor, Luis Urzua, stepped forward and convinced his fellow miners to join together to determine how to make the food they had last and to develop work schedules to keep the miners busy—thereby shifting their attention away from the reality of being trapped thousands of feet underground. Urzua also determined when the lights would go off so that the miners could sleep. He kept the men focused, gave them something to do, and helped them get through their frightening ordeal.

At the conclusion of the miners' triumphant rescue that ended the 69-day ordeal, Chilean President Sebastian Pinera told Urzua, who was the last miner to surface, "You brought your shift out like a good captain."[1] Urzua epitomizes the essence of leadership—the concept of leaders that serve. It is a model that applies similarly to the business world.

Leadership Isn't a Noun, It's a Verb

Marketing must recognize the unique role it has in this new world and lead, not follow. It must welcome accountability and embrace reinvention wholeheartedly. General Colin Powell once said, "Leadership is all about people. It is not about organizations. It is not about plans. It is not about strategies. It is all about people— motivating people to get the job done. You have to be people-centered." He also said, "Trust is the essence of leadership."[1]

Leaders lead. It seems simple, doesn't it? But over the past few years, the term "failure of leadership" has become much more frequently used—in the Gulf region of the United States as the BP oil spill continued unabated, in the financial services industry as the Great Recession took hold, in the automotive industry, in politics—just about everywhere.

What does it take for marketers to avoid a failure of leadership? To my mind, it's simple—it takes both fortitude and boldness.

Embarking on a reinvention strategy is a perilous journey for a marketer. While most truly effective business leaders understand the challenge, this is an era of risk aversion, and there is some risk to reinvention, as there is with all things new. In the end, though, reinvention improves performance and penetration and drives greater and more profitable sales. Therefore, the end does indeed justify the means—as long as marketing delivers.

Great and authentic leaders view accountability as a blessing, not a curse. Leaders motivate teams by setting aspirational goals. Leaders earn the respect of their peers and their people every day, and they never take that respect for granted. Leaders see the future—and change and reinvention—as opportunity. Leaders are passionate about what they do, and everyone can see that and wants to be a part of it.

Leadership Styles

The style of leadership you demonstrate reverberates within the marketing team you create and impacts how the marketing team is viewed both internally and externally. Most important, it can determine whether, as a marketer and reinventer, you are seen as a strategic partner of leadership or a tactical player who simply carries out the directions and orders of others.

In the book *Primal Leadership*, Daniel Goleman, the author of *Emotional Intelligence*, describes six styles of leadership that marketers can use to successfully drive the reinvention of their companies or enterprises. According to a *Wall Street Journal* article on leadership styles:

> The most effective leaders can move among these styles, adopting the one that meets the needs of the moment. They can all become part of the leader's repertoire.

> » **Visionary.** This style is most appropriate when an organization needs a new direction. Its goal is to move people toward a new set of shared dreams. "Visionary leaders articulate where a group is going, but not how it will get there—setting people free to innovate, experiment, [and] take calculated risks," write Mr. Goleman and his coauthors.

>> **Coaching.** This one-on-one style focuses on developing individuals, showing them how to improve their performance, and helping to connect their goals to the goals of the organization. Coaching works best, Mr. Goleman writes, "with employees who show initiative and want more professional development." But it can backfire if it's perceived as "micromanaging" an employee and undermines his or her self-confidence.

>> **Affiliative.** This style emphasizes the importance of team work and creates harmony in a group by connecting people to each other. Mr. Goleman argues this approach is particularly valuable "when trying to heighten team harmony, increase morale, improve communication or repair broken trust in an organization." But he warns against using it alone, since its emphasis on group praise can allow poor performance to go uncorrected. "Employees may perceive," he writes, "that mediocrity is tolerated."

>> **Democratic.** This style draws on people's knowledge and skills and creates a group commitment to the resulting goals. It works best when the direction the organization should take is unclear and the leader needs to tap the collective wisdom of the group. Mr. Goleman warns that this consensus-building approach can be disastrous in times of crisis, when urgent events demand quick decisions.

>> **Pacesetting.** In this style, the leader sets high standards for performance. He or she is "obsessive about doing things better and faster, and asks the same of everyone." But Mr. Goleman warns this style should be used sparingly, because it can undercut morale and make people feel as if they are failing. "Our data show that, more often than not, pacesetting poisons the climate," he writes.

>> **Commanding.** This is classic model of "military" style leadership—probably the most often used, but the least often effective. Because it rarely involves praise and frequently employs criticism, it undercuts morale and job satisfaction. Mr. Goleman argues it is only effective in a crisis, when an urgent turnaround is needed. Even the modern military has come to recognize its limited usefulness.[2]

Leadership Versus Management

The old saying is that leadership is doing the right thing, while management is doing things right. While this saying is only partially true, there is a distinct difference between leadership and management.

The biggest difference is in how you assemble and motivate a team. Leaders get the team to aspire to something more—real reinvention; they are visionaries, and they motivate their people to believe a vision can become reality. Managers inspire their people to meet goals. While they are leaders in their own right, their purview is more limited—usually to the achievement of goals.

Reinventing Leadership

Is it time to reinvent how you as a leader or marketer lead? It may be, depending on your answer to these questions:

>> Is marketing viewed as a strategic partner by leadership?
>> Is marketing part of leadership?
>> Does marketing have a seat at the table when the company's vision and strategy are being set?
>> Does the marketing team consider you someone who creates or quiets and calms drama?
>> Does your team aspire to accomplish the vision you set, or do they think you set the bar too high?
>> Do you see the potential in your team? Leaders accomplish their goals by focusing on potential and reinvention of a brand, products or services, and people.
>> Do your team members know that you always have their back?

If you don't know or can't answer these questions, it's time to reevaluate and then reinvent your management style.

Most important to you, your career, and your team is the sixth rule of reinvention: lead and others will follow. This requires a willingness to reinvent, build, motivate, and drive a team to reach and even exceed its potential; it also means that you will need to demonstrate the following:

>> A willingness to take measured and prudent risks
>> That honesty really is the best policy (Never couch your language for political reasons; giving an honest response is the best way to become a trusted advisor.)
>> That the core values of the company or enterprise have meaning and that you exemplify them

Leadership in the New Paradigm

This book is about more than rules. It is, at its core, about leadership—the role leaders play in companies and enterprises and the leadership role marketers must assume and accept if they are to lead reinvention initiatives. It is in the marketers—their knowledge, outreach, and understanding—that the art of reinvention and the science of marketing join and merge.

Leaders focus on potential. If you understand the core of a product or service, you understand the potential for reinvention and growth. Recognizing and capitalizing on potential means that there are no natural limits to growth, and it assumes that there are no insurmountable barriers to success.

Leaders must focus on the opportunities an economy in transition brings—its potential for change—rather than on the economic disaster that the Great Recession has caused. The Great Recession has left consumers and customers feeling battered and adrift. Their choices, therefore, are driven by necessity and by value. Become their choice by ensuring your key brand differentiators are nourished, refreshed, relevant, and reinvented.

Aspirational Leadership

Leaders focus on aspirational goals—goals your company, organization, or enterprise must stretch to achieve. Create reinvention plans built on aspirational goals, and develop metrics and means for reaching them. Aspirational goals will transform desires to results.

Finally, believe in your aspirations. The force of belief and passion rather than numbers or analysis determines who wins in business. Effective action based on conviction is the basis for groundbreaking results—astonishing things can happen to those who not only persevere, but also have the courage to reinvent.

REMEMBER

- Marketing cannot sit idly by and let others make decisions on customer service, reputation management, pricing, distribution, or the myriad of issues that must be confronted. Marketing must lead.
- Leaders not only inspire, they aspire to more—for their brand, for their team, and for themselves. Visionary leadership begins with aspiration.
- Leaders realize they are only as good as their team, so they create an environment in which their team members can grow, learn, and, when necessary, move on so they can continue their careers.
- Leaders are accountable for their actions—even when they fail. It is strength in the face of adversity that defines a leader.

CONCLUSION

The Essence of Marketing Today

Marketing must reinvent itself—return to its core—if it is to remain relevant in this radically changed, information-rich, and Internet-oriented world.

I t is imperative to recognize that marketing has fundamentally changed. Today, at its core, marketing is different than it was in the late twentieth century. What is the essence of marketing today? It is something that marketers have lost sight of—driving profitable sales, increasing revenues, and creating consumer preference and customer loyalty in a digitally driven and progressively more global marketplace.

Getting Back to the Core

It is time to reinvent the way marketing is practiced, to go back to the core by rewriting many of the rules that have long been followed. This new paradigm has, at its foundation, these fundamentals for reinvention:

Rule One: The Core Is Everything

>> **Principle #1: A Brand's Essence Says It All.** Marketing is all about a brand's core essence. If marketers do not understand that core, or if a brand has grown nonorganically,

revisit the core essence and become better acquainted with its intimate connection to customers, buyers, and targets.

>> **Principle #2: The Customer Really Does Know Best.** Renovation and innovation are overused and often fail. Your products and services must return to their core essence to reinvent these brands based upon consumer and buyer insights and trends to grow revenue profitably and disproportionately.

>> **Principle #3: Your Reputation Precedes You.** Brand management and successful reinvention are inextricably linked to reputation management; if one is at risk, so is the other. Therefore, marketing and communications must work together on clear, consistent messages that can be used to reinvent, define—and immediately defend—the brand.

>> **Principle #4: Play Nicely Together . . . or Else.** Maintaining a brand's core essence in the face of public relations disasters is essential and of great consequence. The relationship between marketing and public relations must be reinvented in a way that protects the core because how a company or enterprise communicates does matter.

>> **Principle #5: Sleep Soundly, Work Fearfully.** The first 10 years of the 21st century have demonstrated that life can change drastically, often in a matter of minutes. As a marketer or communicator, be prepared for the unexpected, and have reinvention plans in place that will work in any situation.

Rule Two: You Have Nothing Without the Foundation

>> **Principle #6: Integrity Is Next to Godliness.** Brand architecture provides the underpinning upon which your brand positioning is built and reinvented. Products and services must be aligned and in support of the company's vision and core to be optimally successful.

>> **Principle #7: A Single Word or Symbol Can Speak Volumes.** Visual impact as part of the brand experience cannot be undervalued. In a world of constant change, companies or enterprises with a strong brand as embodied and personified by their name and logo have an immediate and

lasting connection with the consumer or potential customer. Reinvention begins with the distillation of the core in all elements of brand identity.

» **Principle #8: The Whole Is Larger than Its Parts.** Brand attributes define the personality of a brand—and drive purchase and desire. Knowing these characteristics is of critical importance when determining and reinventing brand positioning.

» **Principle #9: Mind Your P's (and You Can Forget About the A's).** Marketing must drive profitable sales. It does so by understanding how to penetrate the marketplace, its target audience's preferences, and that price-value is more important than price in determining whether a product or service will be bought after it has been reinvented.

» **Principle #10: Do as I Do, Not as I Say.** Recognize that consumers and even customers sometimes say one thing and do another; as a result, it is imperative that marketers use both stated and derived research findings to determine reinvention plans.

Rule Three: There Are Many Choices but Only One Customer

» **Principle #11: Strategy Is the Heart, but Measurement Is the Lifeblood.** Marketing is a data-driven science; to reinvent successfully, you must have a strategic plan with hard metrics that prove return on investment for every dollar spent.

» **Principle #12: Frameworks, Frameworks, Frameworks.** Marketers must be globally consistent in their approach to reinvention and marketing. Frameworks are the most effective way of ensuring this mission is accomplished. and they provide a consistent means for locality-by-locality, state-by-state, country-by-country, and region-by-region comparisons.

» **Principle #13: Perception Really Is Your Customer's Reality.** Reinvention requires reinventing the relationship with a customer until the experience itself has value. How we interact with prospects and customers determines how we are perceived—and perception, in reality, is reality.

» **Principle #14: Communicate; Then Communicate Some More.** As a marketer or communicator, it is your responsibility to keep messages clear, concise, and, most important, consistent. Marketing must then communicate these reinvention-laden messages in as many different ways through as many different channels as it takes to effectively and efficiently reach the target audience, again and again.

» **Principle #15: It's More than Just Channel Surfing.** In the Internet era, communications channels have proliferated, but that doesn't mean that all channels should be used. Strategically review the available digital channels to determine which channels your brand's target audience uses, and exploit these to ensure successful reinvention and better return on investment.

Rule Four: Do the Right Things for the Right Reasons

» **Principle #16: It's All About the Relationship.** Social networks are not the be-all and end-all for marketers undertaking a reinvention initiative. Don't waste time or money marketing through a social network unless marketing has the research and analytics that justify its use and prove it drives profitable sales and increased revenues.

» **Principle #17: You Don't Have to Go It Alone.** Strategic partnerships can be reinvention game changers—but they must be strategically undertaken.

» **Principle #18: It's Not About You, It's Really About Me.** Celebrity endorsements work, but they are a double-edged sword. As long as a company is aware of the dangers and approaches endorsements cautiously, they can be successfully used for reinvention.

» **Principle #19: The Long Arm of the Law.** Regulation and new regulatory bodies directly impact reinvention efforts and the work marketing must do. A company or enterprise can influence the issues, but it must never lose sight of the fact that a crisis, such as the recent Great Recession, can lead to new and unexpected regulations.

Rule Five: Infrastructure Is More than Just Pipes

>> **Principle #20: There's a Reason It's Called the Center.**
Within a marketing organization, there is always tension
between national headquarters and the field. However,
creating a marketing organization that is managed and run
from the center is key to developing an integrated team that
understands not only the reinvention strategy, but also the
context in which it was created. It also provides for marketers to have a seat at the table when important management
decisions are made.

>> **Principle #21: Technology Is Only the Enabler.** Marketers
are often distracted by the latest technology—companies
and enterprises want to be "on it" because it's there, not necessarily because it's appropriate and effective. Technology
enables reinvention, not the other way around.

>> **Principle #22: Right Information, Right People, Right
Time, Wrong Thought.** Thought leadership in all its incar-
nations can be the prized outcome of a reinvention strategy.
It's the upshot and outcome of intense and nonpolitical
internal collaborative processes that can be built on the foundation of reinvention frameworks created by brand managers
and marketing directors.

Rule Six: Lead and Others Will Follow

>> **Principle #23: Leadership Isn't a Noun, It's a Verb.**
Marketing must recognize the unique role it has in this new
digital world and lead, not follow. It must welcome accountability and embrace reinvention wholeheartedly.

Your Role . . . if You Choose to Accept It

Since reinvention is an art that is reliant on a science, it is dependent on its practitioners to change the paradigm. Put bluntly, the
future success of your company or enterprise is up to you. Are
you up to the challenge and reward of reinvention?

NOTES

Introduction

1. Ned Welch, *McKinsey Quarterly*, February 2010, https://www.mc kinseyquarterly.com/marketing/strategy/a_marketers_guide_to _behavioral_economics_2536.

2. *McKinsey Quarterly*, September 2010, https://www.mckinseyquarterly .com/Economic_Studies/Productivity_Performance/Economic_Con ditions_Snapshot_February_2010_McKinsey_Global_Survey_results _2535. The online survey was in the field from September 8 to 13, 2010, and received responses from 2,056 executives representing the full range of regions, industries, tenures, and functional specialties.

Principle #1

1. K. L. Keller, B. Sternthal, and A. Tybout, "Three Questions You Need to Ask About Your Brand," *Harvard Business Review*, September 2002.

2. McKinsey & Company, *Executive Insight*, McKinsey.com, http://www .mckinsey.com/clientservice/marketing/insight.asp.

3. Ben Martin, "Christian Lacroix Goes Bust as Taste for Luxury Dries up," *Times* (London), May 28, 2009, http://business.timesonline.co.uk/ tol/business/industry_sectors/consumer_goods/article6380691.ece.

4. Kevin Almond, updated by Jessica Reisman, "Christian Lacroix," *Fashion Designer Encyclopedia*, http://www.fashionencyclopedia. com/Ki-Le/Lacroix-Christian.html.

5. K. L. Keller, B. Sternthal, and A. Tybout, "Three Questions You Need to Ask About Your Brand," *Harvard Business Review*, September 2002.

6. Ibid.

7. Ibid.

8. Ibid.

9. Ibid.

10. Ibid.

Principle #2

1. Michael George, Anthony Freeling, and Michael Court, "Reinventing the Marketing Organization," *McKinsey Quarterly*, November 1994, https://www.mckinseyquarterly.com/Marketing/Management/Reinventing_the_marketing_organization_64?gp=1.

2. Ibid.

3. *Encarta Dictionary* online, http://encarta.msn.com/encnet/features/dictionary/DictionaryResults.aspx?lextype=3&search=innovation.

4. Stuart Elliot, "Tropicana Discovers Some Consumers Are Passionate About Packaging," *New York Times*, February 22, 2009, http://www.nytimes.com/2009/02/23/business/media/23adcol.html?scp=1&sq=tropicana+advertising&st=nyt.

5. Tom Daykin, "Rival Hot over Chill Sales," *Milwaukee-Wisconsin Journal Sentinel*, July 27, 2007, http://www.jsonline.com/business/29464739.html.

6. John Gurand, "Fox Likes NASCAR's Changes for '10—and How It Made Them," *SportsBusiness Journal*, February 1, 2010, http://www.sportsbusinessjournal.com/article/64740.

7. Jenna Fryer, "NASCAR Deserves Credit for Positive Changes," Yahoo! Sports, May 28, 2010, http://sports.yahoo.com/nascar/news?slug=ap-nascar-inthepits.

8. Charlie Leffler, "Is NASCAR Flat, or Are Fans Losing Interest?" *Richmond Times-Dispatch*, September 10, 2010, http://www2.timesdispatch.com/sports/2010/sep/10/stat10-ar-498003.

9. Sam Black, "Sugar (Free) Rush," Portfolio.com, April 8, 2010, http://www.portfolio.com/companies-executives/2010/04/08/rivals-rush-in-on-cargill-sugar-free-sweetener-truvia#ixzz0lULAlw1i.

10. Justin Scheck and Yukari Iwatani, Kane, "H-P Gambles on Ailing Palm," *Wall Street Journal*, April 29, 2010, http://online.wsj.com/article/SB10001424052748704423504575212503407087936.html?mod=rss_Today's_Most_Popular.

Principle #3

1. Daniel Goldman and Colin Barr, CNNMoney.com, http://money.cnn.com/galleries/2010/news/1006/gallery.ten_hated_companies/11.html.

2. John Aldridge, "I'm Doing 'God's Work'. Meet Mr. Goldman Sachs," *Sunday Times* (London), November 8, 2009, http://www.timesonline .co.uk/tol/news/world/us_and_americas/article6907681.ece.

3. David Ellis, "Dumbest Moments in Business 2009," CNNMoney.com, http://money.cnn.com/galleries/2009/fortune/0912/gallery.dumbest _moments_2009.fortune/index.html.

4. John Aldridge, "I'm Doing 'God's Work'. Meet Mr. Goldman Sachs."

5. Aliyah Shahid, "Goldman Sachs CEO, Lloyd Blankfein, Brags About Pricey Art as Giant Bonus Looms: Report," *New York Daily News*, December 17, 2010, http://www.nydailynews.com/money/2010/12/17/ 2010-12-17_goldman_sachs_ceo_lloyd_blankfein_brags_about_pricey _art_as_giant_bonus_looms_re.html?r=money&utm_source=twitter feed&utm_medium=twitter&utm_campaign=Feed%3A+nydnrss%2F money+%28Money%29.

6. David Ellis, "Dumbest Moments in Business 2009."

7. DealBook (blog), "S.E.C. Accuses Goldman of Fraud in Mortgage Deal," *New York Times*, April 16, 2010, http://dealbook.blogs.nytimes .com/2010/04/16/s-e-c-sues-goldman-over-housing-market-deal/?scp =2&sq=goldman%20sachs%20sec%20&st=cse.

8. Louise Story and Gretchen Morgenston, "S.E.C. Accuses Goldman of Fraud in Housing Deal," *New York Times*, April 16, 2010, http://www .nytimes.com/2010/04/17/business/17goldman.html?dbk.

9. Brian Wingfield, "Goldman Sachs E-Mails Tie Huge Profits to 'Mortgage Mess,'" Forbes.com, April 24, 2010, http://www.forbes.com/2010/ 04/24/goldman-sachs-investigation-senate-lloyd-blankfein-business -washington-goldman.html?boxes=businesschannelsections.

10. Zachary A. Goldfarb, "Goldman Executives Cheered Housing Market's Decline, Newly Released E-mails Show," *Washington Post*, April 25, 2010, http://www.washingtonpost.com/wp-dyn/content/ article/2010/04/24/AR2010042401049.html.

11. Christine Harper, "Goldman's Tourre E-Mail Describes 'Frankenstein' Derivatives," Bloomberg.com, April 24, 2010, http://www.bloomberg .com/apps/news?pid=20601087&sid=aDgzfxGflUMg&pos=2.

12. Nathaniel Popper, "Reports of Criminal Probe Send Goldman Sachs Stock Plunging," *Los Angeles Times*, May 1, 2010, http://articles.latimes .com/2010/may/01/business/la-fi-goldman-20100501.

13. Albert R. Hunt, "Goldman Finds Resume a Pariah with Governments," *BusinessWeek*, April 25, 2010, http://www.businessweek.com/news/ 2010-04-25/goldman-finds-resume-a-pariah-with-governments-albert -r-hunt.html.

14. Felix Salmon, "With SEC Charges, Goldman Sachs's Reputation Is Tarnished," *Washington Post*, April 25, 2010, http://www.washington post.com/wp-dyn/content/article/2010/04/23/AR2010042303780.html.

Principle #4

1. Peter Goodman, "In Case of Emergency, What Not to Do," *New York Times*, August 21, 2010, http://www.nytimes.com/2010/08/22/business/22crisis.html?pagewanted=1&_r=1&sq=public relations&st=cse&scp=2.
2. Ibid.
3. Ibid.
4. Nathan Schock, "Handling a Fake Twitter Account: @BPGlobalPR Leaves Lasting Impression on Crisis Communications," *PR Strategist*, August 23, 2010, http://www.prsa.org/intelligence/thestrategist/articles/view/8757/1019/handling_a_fake_twitter_account_bpglobalpr_leaves?utm_campaign=PRSASearch&utm_source=PRSAWebsite&utm_medium=SSearch&utm_term=crisis%20communications.
5. Ibid.
6. Ibid.
7. Eric Jackson, "H-P's Hurd's Expenses Have Been Troubling for Three Years Now," Breakout Performance (blog), August 6, 2010, http://breakoutperformance.blogspot.com/2010/08/h-ps-hurds-expenses-have-been-troubling.html.
8. Connie Guglielmo, Ian King, and Aaron Ricadela, "HP Chief Executive Hurd Resigns After Sexual-Harassment Probe," *BusinessWeek*, August 7, 2010, http://www.businessweek.com/news/2010-08-07/hp-chief-executive-hurd-resigns-after-sexual-harassment-probe.html.
9. DealBook (blog), "Oracle Chief Faults H.P. Board for Forcing Hurd Out," *New York Times*, August 9, 2010, http://dealbook.blogs.nytimes.com/2010/08/09/oracle-chief-faults-h-p-board-for-forcing-hurd-out/?scp=6&sq=H.P.%20and%20ellison&st=Search.
10. Ashlee Vance, "Hurd Is Now a President at Oracle, H.P.'s Rival," *New York Times*, September 7, 2010, http://query.nytimes.com/gst/fullpage.html?res=9402E5DD1531F934A3575AC0A9669D8B63&scp=17&sq=H.P.%20and%20ellison&st=Search.
11. Ashlee Vance, "H.P. Sues Its Ex-Chief in New Job," *New York Times*, September 7, 2010, http://www.nytimes.com/2010/09/08/technology/08hewlett.html?scp=20&sq=H.P.%20and%20ellison&st=Search.

Principle #5

1. Ian Davis, "The New Normal," *McKinsey Quarterly*, March 2009, https://www.mckinseyquarterly.com/the_new_normal_2326.

2. Associated Press, "Ford Distances Itself from Bailout Proposal," December 10, 2008, msnbc.com http://www.msnbc.msn.com/id/28159257.

3. "Hanging Up On Dell?" *BusinessWeek*, October 10, 2005, http://www.businessweek.com/magazine/content/05_41/b3954102.htm.

4. Ibid.

5. Ibid.

6. Louise Lee, "It's Bad to Worse at Dell," *BusinessWeek*, November 1, 2005, http://www.businessweek.com/technology/content/nov2005/tc20051101_088420.htm.

7. Ashlee Vance, "Suit Over Faulty Computers Highlights Dell's Decline," *New York Times*, June 28, 2010, http://www.nytimes.com/2010/06/29/technology/29dell.html?_r=1&scp=1&sq=dell%20optiplex%20lawsuit&st=cse.

Principle #6

1. Romulo Sanchez Rajagopal, "Conceptual Analysis of Brand Architecture and Relationships Within Product Categories," *Journal of Brand Management* (2004) 11: 233–247.

2. Prophet (company), "Brand Portfolio and Brand Architecture in Single Brand Companies," posted February 22, 2010, http://www.prophet.com/downloads/articles/product-architecture.pdf.

3. "Session Four: Understanding Brand Architecture," Brand 2.0 Advanced Brand Strategy Masterclass 2007, http://www.slideshare.net/imootee/brand-masterclass-week-four.

4. Michael Watkins, "Job 1 at GM," Blogs, *Harvard Business Review*, June 1, 2009, http://blogs.hbr.org/watkins/2009/06/job_1_at_gm.html.

5. Ibid.

Principle #7

1. Dennis Hahn, "Branding from Inside Out," allaboutbranding.com, http://www.allaboutbranding.com/index.lasso?article=428#foot.

2. Amanda Baltazar, "News Analysis: Silly Brand Names Get Serious Attention," *Brandweek*, December 3, 2008, http://www.brandweek.com/bw/esearch/article_display.jsp?vnu_content_id=1003679909.

3. Veronica Napoles, *Corporate Identity Design* (New York, NY: Van Nostrand Reinhold, 1988).

4. Dinesh.com, "Nike Logo—Design and History," http://www.dinesh.com/history_of_logos/miscellaneous_logos_-_design_and_history/nike_logo_-_design_and_history.html.

5. Pauline Hammerbeck, "Decade of Design," *Brand Packaging*, September 1, 2010, http://www.brandpackaging.com/Articles/Cover_Story/BNP_GUID_9-5-2006_A_10000000000000893382.

6. Amy McManus, "Brand Compliance Essential to Protect Your Company's Emotional Connection to Customers," Brandchannel, http://www.brandchannel.com/papers_review.asp?sp_id=1262.

Principle #8

1. David Johnston and John Broder, "FBI Says Guards Killed 14 Iraqis Without Cause," *New York Times*, November 14, 2007, http://www.nytimes.com/2007/11/14/world/middleeast/14blackwater.html?_r=2.

2. Eric Wilson, "Why Does This Pair of Pants Cost $550?" *New York Times*, April 29, 2010, http://www.nytimes.com/2010/04/29/fashion/29ROW.html?hpw.

3. Natalie Mizik and Robert Jacobson, "How Brand Attributes Drive Financial Results" (working paper), Marketing Science Institute, 2005, http://www.msi.org/publications/publication.cfm?pub=856.

4. Floyd Norris, "Did Wall Street Blow It Again?" Floyd Norris: Notions on High and Low Finance (blog), *New York Times*, April 20, 2010, http://norris.blogs.nytimes.com/2010/04/20/did-wall-street-blow-it-again/?scp=1&sq=Did%20Wall%20Street%20Blow%20It%20Again?&st=cse.

5. Peter J. Henning, "What's Next for Goldman Sachs?" DealBook (blog), *New York Times*, April 29, 2010, http://dealbook.blogs.nytimes.com/2010/04/29/whats-next-for-goldman-sachs/?scp=3&sq=goldman%20sachs&st=cse.

6. Gretchen Morgenson and Louise Story, "Clients Worried About Goldman's Dueling Goals," *New York Times*, May 18, 2010, http://www.nytimes.com/2010/05/19/business/19client.html?scp=4&sq=goldman%20sachs&st=cse.

7. Ibid.

Principle #9

1. I believe this was originally used at Coca-Cola marketing in the 1980s; it was also used by Zyman Group, the marketing consulting firm that I led, during my time there as president and CEO (2005–2007).

2. Alex Dobuzinskis, "Movie Studios Try to Harness 'Twitter Effect,'" Reuters, July 17, 2009, http://www.reuters.com/article/idUSTRE56G74 H20090717.

3. Stephanie Clifford, "Linking Customer Loyalty with Social Networking," *New York Times*, April 28, 2010, http://www.nytimes.com/2010/04/29/ business/media/29adco.html?ref=business.

4. James Anderson and Lee Rainie, "Future of the Internet IV," Pew Internet & American Life Project, February 19, 2010, http://www.pew internet.org/Reports/2010/Future-of-the-Internet-IV.aspx.

5. Miguel Helft and Ashlee Vance, "Apple Passes Microsoft as No. 1 in Tech," *New York Times*, May 26, 2010, http://www.nytimes.com/2010/ 05/27/technology/27apple.html?sq=apple&st=cse&scp=2&page wanted=print.

6. Ibid.

7. *New York Times*, "Apple Delays International Release of iPad," April 14, 2010, http://www.nytimes.com/2010/04/15/technology/15apple.html ?scp=1&sq=apple%20international%20delay&st=cse.

8. Miguel Helft and Ashlee Vance, "Apple Passes Microsoft as No. 1 in Tech."

9. Saul Hansell, "Why AT&T Wants to Keep the iPhone Away from Verizon," Bits (blog), *New York Times*, April 22, 2009, http://bits.blogs .nytimes.com/2009/04/22/why-att-wants-to-keep-the-iphone-away-from -verizon/?scp=12&sq=apple%20and%20at&t&st=Search.

10. Ibid.

11. Miquel Helft, "Apple Plans to Offer iPhone on Verizon," *New York Times*, October 8, 2010.

12. Reuters, "AT&T to Buy Qualcomm's Mobile Spectrum for $1.93 Billion," December 20, 2010.

13. David Pogue, "New Kindle Leaves Rivals Further Back," *New York Times*, August 25, 2010, http://www.nytimes.com/2010/08/26/technology/ personaltech/26pogue.html.

14. Michael Gartenberg, "Apple's Secret Weapon: Consumer Education," Macworld, May 27, 2010, http://www.macworld.com/article/151606/2010/ 05/gartenberg_ipad.html.

15. Ibid.

16. Mark Brandau, "Taste, Convenience Drives Restaurant Purchases," *Nation's Restaurant News*, April 14, 2010, http://www.nrn.com/article .aspx?menu_id=1368&id=382122#ixzz0lUeu4hCS.

17. Ibid.

18. Joint Economic Committee of the U.S. Senate and House of Representatives report, "Women in the Recession: Working Mothers Face High Rates of Unemployment," May 28, 2009, http://maloney.house .gov/index.php?option=com_content&task=view&id=1855&Itemid=61.

19. Brian Stelter, "NBC-Comcast Deal Puts Broadcast TV in Doubt," *New York Times*, December 6, 2009, http://www.nytimes.com/2009/ 12/07/business/media/07nbc.html?_r=1&scp=3&sq=comcast+and+nbc &st=nyt.

Principle #10

1. Tara Parker-Pope, "Surprisingly, Family Time Has Grown," Well (blog), *New York Times*, April 5, 2010, http://well.blogs.nytimes.com/2010/ 04/05/surprisingly-family-time-has-grown/?scp=18&sq=time&st=cse.

2. Valerie Bauerlein and Chris Herring, "Bloomberg Wins Re-Election in New York City," *Wall Street Journal*, November 5, 2009, A4.

3. David Chen and Michael Barbaro, "Bloomberg Wins 3rd Term as Mayor in Unexpectedly Close Race," *New York Times*, November 3, 2009, http://www.nytimes.com/2009/11/04/nyregion/04mayor.html.

4. John Greenwald, "Coca-Cola's Big Fizzle," *Time*, April 12, 2005, http:// www.time.com/time/magazine/article/0,9171,1048370-3,00.html#ixzz 12Yv27YhI.

5. The Coca-Cola Company, "Coke Lore: The Real Story of New Coke," http://www.thecocacolacompany.com/heritage/cokelore_newcoke.html.

Principle #11

1. Sears Archives, "Sears History—1980 to Today," http://www.sears archives.com/history/history1980s.htm.

2. Wikipedia, "Marketing Research Process," http://en.wikipedia.org/ wiki/Marketing_research_process.

3. Steve Tobak, "Is Brand Loyalty Dead?" The Corner Office (blog), BNET.com, February 18, 2010, http://blogs.bnet.com/ceo/?p=3852.

4. Duff Wilson, "Pfizer to Cut Researchers in Preparation for Lipitor Patent Expiration," *New York Times*, January 4, 2009.

Principle #13

1. http://www.youtube.com/watch?v=CvVp7b5gzqU.

2. Brad Tuttle, "The Reward for Bad Customer Service," It's Your Money (blog), *Time*, August 23, 2010, http://money.blogs.time.com/2010/08/23/the-reward-for-bad-customer-service.

3. Dana Mattioli, "Customer Service as a Growth Engine," *Wall Street Journal*, June 7, 2010, http://online.wsj.com/article/SB100014240527487 04080104575287153987995176.html?KEYWORDS=%22knowledge+man agement%22.

4. Associated Press, "Woman Gets Cable Bill with Derogatory Name," August 18, 2005, http://www.msnbc.msn.com/id/9001509.

5. Rick Germano, "Comcast: We May Not Always Get it Right, But We're Trying," *Advertising Age*, December 17, 2007, http://adage.com/article ?article_id=122660.

6. Comcast, "Comcast Customer Guarantee," http://www.comcast.com/Corporate/Customers/CustomerGuarantee.html.

7. Neely Tucker, "Taking a Whack Against Comcast," *Washington Post*, October 18, 2007, http://www.washingtonpost.com/wp-dyn/content/article/2007/10/17/AR2007101702359.html.

8. James Surowiecki, "Are You Being Served?" *New Yorker*, September 6, 2010, http://www.newyorker.com/talk/financial/2010/09/06/100906ta_talk_surowiecki.

9. Erica Ogg, "Secrets of Apple's Customer Success," CNET News, September 21, 2010, http://edition.cnn.com/2010/TECH/mobile/09/21/cnet.apple.customer.service.

10. Jeremy Toeman, "The Real Secret of Apple's Product Philosophy," Cult of Mac, September 21, 2010, www.cultofmac.com/the-real-secret-of -apple%E2%80%99s-product-philosophy-opinion/60078.

11. James Surowiecki, "Are You Being Served?"

12. Robert Spector and Patrick D. McCarthy, *The Nordstrom Way: The Inside Story of America's #1 Customer Service Company*, (New York, NY: Wiley & Sons, 1995).

13. Jay Goltz, "Why Customer Service Is So Bad," You're the Boss (blog), *New York Times*, August 4, 2009, http://boss.blogs.nytimes.com/2009/08/04/why-customer-service-is-so-bad/?scp=7&sq=customer%20 service&st=cse.

Principle #14

1. Louise Story and Gretchen Morgenston, "S.E.C. Accuses Goldman of Fraud in Mortgage Deal," *New York Times*, April 16, 2010, http://www.nytimes.com/2010/04/17/business/17goldman.html?dbk.

2. Laurent Belsie, "With Tylenol Recall 2010, a Corporate Icon Stumbles," *Christian Science Monitor*, January 15, 2010, http://www.csmonitor.com/Money/new-economy/2010/0115/With-Tylenol-recall-2010-a-corporate-icon-stumbles.

3. Melly Alazraki, "Johnson & Johnson's Tylenol Recall Woes Are Getting Worse," DailyFinance, May 20, 2010, http://www.dailyfinance.com/story/company-news/tylenol-recall-update/19483610/#.

4. Ibid.

5. Reuters, "Timeline: Toyota Warned of Floormat Risk Since 2007," March 25, 2010.

6. Ibid.

7. Chris Woodyard, "Toyota Fined Another $32 million for Safety Reporting Lapses," *USA Today*, December 20, 2010.

8. Louise Story and Julie Creswell, "For Bank of America and Merrill, Love Was Blind," *New York Times*, February 7, 2009, http://www.nytimes.com/2009/02/08/business/08split.html.

9. Ibid.

Principle #15

1. McClatchy Newspapers, "Founder of Geek Squad Is Best Buy's Corporate Visionary," *Richmond Times-Dispatch*, April 5, 2010.

2. Ibid.

3. Peter Overby, "The Fate of Obama's Net Roots Network," All Things Considered blog, December 2, 2008, http://www.npr.org/templates/story/story.php?storyId=97722217.

4. Liz Sidoti, "AP-GfK Poll: Standing Slips for Obama, Democrats," April 14, 2010, Associated Press, http://www.google.com/hostednews/ap/article/ALeqM5ieRl-aeFR6tUPV_ChEXYfIMNmCRgD9F30QJ00.

5. Ibid.

6. Jennifer Steinhauer, "Short and Sweet—A Candidate's Twitter Announcement," April 21, 2009, The Caucus (blog), *New York Times*, http://thecaucus.blogs.nytimes.com/2009/04/21/short-and-sweet-a-candidates-twitter-announcement.

Principle #16

1. Brian Morrissey, "Does Social Sell?" *Brandweek*, February 14, 2010, http://www.brandweek.com/bw/content_display/esearch/e3i82693d9 fec5d7f343bc1bf14d81004ef.

2. Ibid.

3. Ibid.

4. Josh Bernoff, "Why You Should Advertise on Twitter," *Advertising Age*, April 13, 2010, http://adage.com/digitalnext/article?article_id =143257.

5. "Jon Stewart on *Crossfire*: 'Stop, Stop, Stop, Stop Hurting America,'" Media Matters for America (blog), October 15, 2004, http://media matters.org/research/200410160003.

6. "'Hardball with Chris Matthews' for Friday, July 25[, 2008]" (transcript), MSNBC, http://www.msnbc.msn.com/id/25885493/.html.

7. Bill Carter, "Beyond Larry King, Ratings Declines for CNN Programs," Media Decoder (blog), *New York Times*, June 30, 2010, http://media decoder.blogs.nytimes.com/2010/06/30/beyond-larry-king-ratings -declines-for-cnn-programs/?scp=2&sq=CNN%20ratings&st=Search.

8. Brian Stelter, "CNN Fires Executive Who Led Makeover," *New York Times*, September 24, 2010, http://www.nytimes.com/2010/09/25/busi ness/media/25cnn.html?ref=business.

9. General Electric (website), http://www.ge.com.

10. Mark Dolliver (*Adweek*), "Consumers Feel Loyalty Programs Hold 'Little' Value," *Brandweek*, February 16, 2010, http://www.brandweek .com/bw/content_display/esearch/e3i4a73f5d7451749a36704e6d604 57d7da.

Principle #17

1. Damon Hack, "McCormack and Palmer Changed the World of Sports and Business Forever," Golf.com, December 16, 2008, http://www.golf .com/golf/tours_news/article/0,28136,1866427,00.html.

Principle #18

1. Bob Greene, "Are Celebrity Endorsements Worthless?" CNN.com, April 4, 2010, http://www.cnn.com/2010/OPINION/04/04/greene.endorsements .celebrities/index.html.

2. Ibid.

3. A. K. Cabell, "Celebrity Endorsements Reach for the Stars," Brand channel.com, June 2, 2003, http://www.brandchannel.com/features _effect.asp?pf_id=160.

4. Ibid.

5. WikiInvest Stock Analysis, "Nike (NKE)," http://www.wikinvest.com/ stock/Nike_(NKE)#Equipment_.286.25_of_Revenue.29.

6. Steve McKee, "The Trouble with Celebrity Endorsements," Viewpoint, *BusinessWeek*, November 14, 2008, http://www.businessweek.com/ smallbiz/content/nov2008/sb20081114_106175.htm.

7. T. L. Stanley, "Year of the Tiger," *Brandweek*, March 7, 2010, http:// www.brandweek.com/bw/content_display/esearch/e3id2f310d328e5e6 6c7cc809c3bf115d77.

8. Nanci Hellmich, "Sarah Ferguson: Weight Watchers' Royal Spokes-woman," *USA Today*, updated May 12, 2009, http://www.usatoday.com/ news/health/weightloss/2008-03-11-dieter-ferguson_N.htm.

Principle #19

1. Ian Davis, "The New Normal," *McKinsey Quarterly*, March 2009, https://www.mckinseyquarterly.com/The_new_normal_2326.

2. Sean Tucker, "Auto Bailout," *US News & World Report*, July 20, 2008, http://usnews.rankingsandreviews.com/cars-trucks/Auto-Bailout.

3. Eric Lichtblau and Eric Dash, "Goldman and Its Lobbyists Spurned in Fight on Bill," *New York Times*, April 28, 2010, http://www.nytimes .com/2010/04/29/business/29lobby.html?src=mv.

4. Reuters, "TIMELINE—Gulf of Mexico Oil Spill,"updated June 3, 2010, http://www.reuters.com/article/idUSN0322326220100603?type=markets News.

5. Frederic J. Frommer, "Revolving Door Between BP and Its Regulator Getting More Attention," *Huffington Post*, May 26, 2010, http://www .huffingtonpost.com/2010/05/26/bp-revolving-door-interior_n_591040 .html?view=print.

6. "MMS's Troubled Past," *Washington Post*, May 29, 2010, http://www .washingtonpost.com/wp-dyn/content/article/2010/05/28/AR20100 52804599.html?hpid=topnews&sid=ST2010052805077.

Principle #20

1. Donald Sull, "Competing Through Organizational Agility," *McKinsey Quarterly*, December 2009, https://www.mckinseyquarterly.com/Com peting_through_organizational_agility_2488.

2. Giancarlo Ghislanzoni, Risto Penttinen, and David Turnbull, "The Multilocal Challenge: Managing Cross-Border Functions," *McKinsey Quarterly*, March 2008, https://www.mckinseyquarterly.com/The _multilocal_challenge_Managing_cross-border_functions_2116.

Principle #21

1. Brian Stelter, "Honoring Citizen Journalists," *New York Times*, February 21, 2010, http://www.nytimes.com/2010/02/22/business/ media/22polk.html.

2. Jon Swartz, "Library of Congress to Archive All Public Twitter Tweets," *USA Today*, April 14, 2010, http://www.usatoday.com/tech/news/2010-04 -14-library-congress-twitter_N.htm.

3. Ibid.

4. David Kiley and Burt Helm, "The Short Life of the Chief Marketing Officer," *BusinessWeek*, November 29, 2007, http://www.businessweek .com/magazine/content/07_50/b4062063789246_page_2.htm.

5. Kristin Schweitzer, "U.S. Web Advertising Exceeds Newspaper Print Ads in 2010, eMarketer Says," Bloomberg.net, December 20, 2010.

6. Shira Ovide and Yukari Iwatani Kane, "Apple Coaxes Publishers to Join It on iPad Subscriptions," *Wall Street Journal*, September 20, 2010, http://online.wsj.com/article/SB100014240527487044169045755019 12896373130.html.

7. MarketingSavant and CinCom, "Tools and Trends in Marketing Technology: The MarkeTech Guide to Marketing Technology and Social Media Marketing," 2009 http://expertaccess.cincom.com/wp -content/uploads/2009/10/Marketech_Final_wCinacomLogo.pdf.

8. Forrester Research, February 2009.

Principle #22

1. Meridith Levinson, "Knowledge Management Definition and Solutions," CIO, http://www.cio.com/article/40343/Knowledge_Management _Definition_and_Solutions?page=1.

2. Ibid.

3. Paul B. Brown, "Getting the Most Out of the Human Asset," *New York Times*, February 19, 2008, http://www.nytimes.com/2008/02/19/business/19toolkit.html?_r=1&scp=5&sq=%22knowledge%20management%22&st=cse.

4. Meridith Levinson, "Knowledge Management Definition and Solutions."

5. "Gartner Says Thought Leadership Marketing Can Be a Powerful Tool for IT Services Providers" (press release), Gartner Newsroom, February 1, 2010, http://www.gartner.com/it/page.jsp?id=1292013.

6. McKinsey & Co. North American Knowledge Center, "The McKinsey Way," http://www.siliconyogi.com/andreas/it_professional/NAKC/The McKinseyWay.html. Knowledge management history taken from this site, which presents an overview of the book *The McKinsey Way*.

7. Fiona Czerniawska, "Do Strategy Firms Still Lead the Thinking?" *Management Consulting News*, http://www.managementconsulting news.com/articles/czerniawska_strat_firm.php.

Rule Six

1. Chris Kraul, "Chile Rejoices as All 33 Miners Are Rescued," *Los Angeles Times*, October 14, 2010, latimes.com http://articles.latimes.com/2010/oct/14/world/la-fg-chile-miner-rescues-20101014.

Principle #23

1. Govleaders.org http://govleaders.org/quotes.htm.

2. "Leadership Styles" (adapted from Alan Murray, *The Wall Street Journal Guide to Management*, published by Harper Business), http://guides.wsj.com/management/developing-a-leadership-style/how-to-develop-a-leadership-style.

INDEX

ABOUT THE AUTHOR

Timothy **R. Pearson** is founder and president of Pearson Advisors || Partners, a marketing management consulting firm serving *Fortune 1000* and brand-driven clients requiring business strategy and planning, mergers and acquisitions analysis, brand strategy and value proposition development, go-to-market activation, and business and brand analytics.

Tim is a highly sought advisor to senior management and a frequent keynote speaker at industry conferences, at leadership meetings, and on the lecture circuit. He has served as president and CEO of Zyman Group, a leading international management consulting firm, and as Vice Chair, Global Managing Partner, Marketing and Communications (and first Chief Marketing Officer) for KPMG, the global Big 4 accounting, tax, and consulting firm. Earlier in his career he was president of several award-winning advertising agencies, where he led initiatives for and within a number of the world's leading companies.

Pearson is often quoted by newspapers and commentators. He has written articles for *Brandweek* magazine and lectured before numerous audiences and members of the American Marketing Association on topics ranging from "Do or Die: The Reinvention of Marketing," "Out of the Blue: A Global Brand Defined," "The Value of Leadership and Business Ethics," "The M&M Factor," "Machiavelli on Global Branding," "Top of Mind: Product or Service Focus Must Be Clear," and "Competitive Positioning by Cable Television Against the Networks."

Tim Pearson has served on the Advisory Board of the Nobel Peace Center, Oslo, Norway, and on the Harvard Business School's Dean's Research Society. He has received numerous honors in the marketing arena, including but not limited to Advertising Age's Best, The Wall Street Journal's Best, and multiple Belding, Cable, Clio, Echo, Golden Phone, Lulu, Proto, PRSA, and Sunny awards.

Pearson is also the cocreator of numerous interactive games and was issued U.S. Patent #5,018,736, "Interactive Game System and Method;" U.S. Patent #5,263,723, "Interactive Contest System;" and Canada Patent #2,044,266, "Interactive Game System and Method."

Tim received his B.A. in English Literature from DePauw University where he was a Maxwell Scholar. He currently resides in Atlanta, Georgia, and Saddle River, New Jersey.

At the author's Web site, www.pearsonadvisorsandpartners .com, you can access additional material on the subject of the new rules of marketing, read recent articles he has written, and learn more about emerging technologies and trends. For speaking engagements, please contact Peter Jacobs at CAA Speakers at 424-288-2898 or speakers@caa.com. Please contact the author with comments or queries at timrp@aol.com.

Your Online Bookstore

5750 Campbell Rd
Houston, TX, 77041, USA

Packing slip for AmazonUS order 107-8720526-5306648 (this IS NOT a bill)

Order Date: Feb 14 2015
Shipping Service: standard
Shipping To: ROBERT ESSIG
                 51603 HENDON HALL CT
                 GRANGER, IN, 46530-8348

Product Details	Price
Title: The Old Rules of Marketing are Dead: 6 New Rules to Reinvent Your Brand and Reignite Your Business [Paperback] [2011] Pearson, Timothy R.	
ISBN: 0071788220 **SKU:** GNT6834EMPA03272014H15794C	$0.01
Condition: New - New **Quantity:** 1	
Comments: Unbeatable customer service, and we usually ship the same or next day. Over one million satisfied customers!	

Subtotal:	$0.01
Shipping & Handling:	$3.99
Tax:	$0.00
Total:	$4.00

5676020XW; 0+0 EMPA??

Thank you for your order! If you have any questions or concerns, please feel free to contact us directly at customerservice@youronlinebookstore.com.